Answers

To A

Pool Player's

Prayers

Answers

To A

Pool Player's

Prayers

By Richard Kranicki

**Edited by
Barbara Home Stewart**

Hand illustrations by **Dennie Ward**

Computer drawings and front cover design by **Joe Bede**

Mosconi photo retouched by Joseph A. Purul III

Copyright © 2000 by Richard Kranicki
All rights reserved.
No Part of this book may be reproduced or transmitted in any form or by any means, electronic or mechanical, including photocopying, recording, or by any information storage and retrieval system, without written permission of the publisher.

ISBN: 1-58820-445-6

For additional copies of this book or to contact the author, write:

Richard Kranicki
Pool Eyes Publications
247 Dickinson Street
Philadelphia, Pa. 19147-6003

Library of Congress Cataloguing in Publication Data
Richard Kranicki
Answers To A Pool Player's Prayers
First Publishing, June 1999 by Pool Eyes Publications
Printed in the United States of America

1stBooks – rev. 9/26/00

Acknowledgments

Special thanks to my mother, **Rita Kranicki**, for all the years of understanding and support. Without her help my "seemingly endless" work would have been delayed for several more years.

Thanks to **Barbara Home Stewart** for her caring advice and friendly encouragement and for showing me the "Artist's Way". Barbara's professional and friendly empathy has helped me to weather some thunderous storms.

A sentimental thanks to **Mrs. Mildred Hanak**, my first Drama Coach, for helping me to develop my imagination. Mildred is the first person to tell me that I have a talent for writing. She continues to remind me that "belief is the fuel".

A commemorative thanks to the late **Willie Mosconi** for the inspiration that sparked "The Beginning". To Mrs. **Flora Mosconi** for giving me a chance.

Thanks to **Helson** and **Carol Meirino** for being my friendly "sounding boards" for all these years.

Thanks to my friend **Joe Bede** of The Printing Office, Inc. for his ideas, help, input and all the computer lessons.

Thanks to **Jerry Briesath** - The Pool School - for being the first person to teach me the "correct" basics. His enthusiasm was and still is contagious.

Thanks to **Sven Davies** for his interest and help in making some important contacts.

And Infinite Thanks to ***The Holy Father, The Holy Son*** and ***The Holy Spirit*** for the Special Gifts of *Curiosity*, *Wonderment*, *Imagination*, *Patience*, *Discipline*, *Faith* and *Perseverance* which helped me to do my best.

Table of Contents

Aiming Methods 1
    The Imaginary Cue Ball Method 2
    Double the Distance Method 4
    Contact to Contact Method 7
    Willie Mosconi 9

Pool Eyes 11

Straight Shooting Test 13
    Light Reflection 16
    Off-Centered Light Reflection 18

ALIGNMENT 21
    Peripheral Sighting 21
    Focal Point 21
    Equi-angled and Equidistant Eyes 22
    Straight Head 23
    Turned Head 24
    Tilted Head 25
    Turned and Tilted Head 26
    Mirror Aid 28
    Guide Points 31
    Footing in Alignment 33
    Big Toe 34
    Left Eye Point 35
    Pure Eye Aim 36
    Right Eye Point 37
    Front Foot 38

Outward - Inward Eyesight Angles 41
    Five Objects to Aim 42
    Outward-Looking-In Angles 42
    Line of Sight 43
    Intersection 44
    Three Different Facial Guidepoints 46
    Focusing 48
    Fictitious Eye 49

Aiming The Cue Ball 51
    The Aim Starting Point 51
    Top Guide Point 53
    Eye Switching 61
    Recalibrate 62
    Dominant Eye 63

  Peripheral Vision 64

Aim Compensation 67
  Balanced Aim 68
  Dominant Eye Alignment 75
  Inferior Eye 76

The Real Cue Ball Center 77
  Apparent Center 77
  Front Center Point 82
  Top Vertical Point 83
  Whole Cue Ball Centerline 84
  Synchronized Peripheral Aim 87

Cue Tip Aim Compensation 89
  ½ Cue Tip Point 90
  ¼ Cue Tip Point 91
  ⅛ Cue Tip Point 92

Applications 95
  Cue Tip Compensation/Double the Distance 95
  Imaginary Cue Ball/Vertical Bottom Center Point 96
  Alignment 97
  Aiming 98
  Parallel Aiming 99
  Pure Eye Parallel Aim 100
  Two Eye parallel Aim 101

LOOK OUT BELOW! 105
  Real Equator Line 105
  Apparent Top/Bottom Points 106
  Real Top/Bottom Points 106
  Standing View 107
  Apparent Equator Line 109
  Apparent Object Ball Contact Point 109
  Visual Bisecting 109
  Below the Real Equator Line 113

PREFACE

After years of tirelessly studying all the available instructional pool books, watching pool videos, spending thousands of hours of scrutinizing high staked money matches between Top Gun players (live and on videos), and donating thousands of my hard earned dollars for professional lessons, I learned a lot regarding pool. Unfortunately, it just wasn't enough. Painfully, I had come to realize that many of my original questions concerning the alignment and the aiming of two spherical shaped balls were still.... UNANSWERED!

Eventually, it became evident to me that the historical instructions, which made a very small percent of the pool populace into world and national class players, were not producing the same results for me. I'm sorry to say that the good-natured motivational advice like.... "It will happen" and "Relax, don't shoot until your ready".... did little to improve my game. Yep! For me there was no disputing.... I needed a different approach with germinating fruits.

Jimmy Fusco, an all around world-class pool player and a strong Billiard player, with all his decades of accumulated experience and instincts, told me that he loses about 50% of his feel for the game when he doesn't play for three days. **Pete Fusco**, Jimmy's cousin and another all around world-class pool player, said, *"even when you know what to do; it is still very hard to do it consistently"*. Pool is a very demanding sport requiring an enormous amount of thought, practice and playing. I know there is validity in the words - "practice makes perfect", but when I kept failing to reach my self-expected goals, I knew that the 'what and how' to practice would have to get all my focus.

A recent magazine poll stated that over 200 million people play pool. Well, I will speculate that the number of world, national and state-class players are probably a couple million, or so. That leaves at least 95% of the pool population who can still use some realistic improvement in their game.

We all have limits, but can anyone say that the bulk of the pool population is playing anywhere close to their true potential? Are we only using 10% of our pool brain capabilities?

Thousands of players quit playing pool, because they felt that they were not able to improve their game, after investing a lot of their time, money and energy. Tens of thousands of disappointed 'one-nighters' carelessly surrendered their borrowed or rented house-cues after prematurely deciding that pool was too hard to 'get into'.

There must be tens of millions players with average intelligence who have been diligently playing pool for years, but are somewhat disappointed, because they are not playing the level of pool suitable to their personal potential and expectations. I see it all the time; amateurs and advanced players struggling to make a straight shot.

Today's pool player and fans are highly sophisticated. They appreciate and welcome honest attempts to expand their understanding and enjoyment of pool. I'm convinced that they desire the mere satisfaction of seeing their practice pay earlier dividends in their game, besides searching for an 'edge' over their competition, without becoming unnecessarily psychotic with frustration.

After a couple of years into my 'private exploring', I found myself in one of the greatest relationships I could ever hope to enjoy with the person whom many people regard as the finest pool player of all time - the late **Willie Mosconi**.

It was a rare and unique privilege to have some of my ideas evaluated by the **Grand Master** himself. It was our intention to work together to produce a refreshing type of instructional pool book. Sadly, **Willie** passed away before this collaboration started.

However, the purpose of my writing this book, now, is to share the intriguing innovations that I unearthed during the ransacking of my imagination. It is meant to encourage players of all levels to let their individual imaginations spawn new ideas of their own. This book, also, reveals that before you can align, stroke, and aim straight.... YOU MUST SEE STRAIGHT.

Straight Alignment, straight Stroking and straight Aiming together make up this book's pool shooting package. Knowledge of any separate one, or of any two of the three, results in an incomplete study. You must have an understanding of each one, in order to see how they affect each other. They all work together.

So, it is my sincere hope that my **ANSWERS TO A POOL PLAYER'S PRAYERS** will appeal to the curiosity, competitive spirit and meet the heartwarming approval of the 95%.

Aiming Methods

Aiming is the phase of pool that tormented me for a number of years. In spite of the several ways that I was taught, my shot making ability suffered inconsistencies. After practicing the different methods for a couple of years, I still could not develop confidence when shooting a thin cut shot or the long shot. I realized something was missing for me, but I didn't know what. (No! I didn't need glasses).

I searched all the available instructional pool books and pool tapes that I could buy or borrow. I even went against my better judgment by sending my money to the suspicious looking magazine ads, which claimed they had the "secret of aiming" for sale. I studied with a few of the famous instructors in the United States; hoping that they would satisfy my starving curiosity. I hounded several different world class, national class and state class pool players, hoping to get them to reveal their magical aiming secrets. But after all their cue chalk dust settled, I still wasn't fully satisfied.

Why didn't the same methods produce the same results for me as the better players? Why wasn't I able to make the shots that I was making, more consistently?

Every time I shot a straight shot, I was reminded that the instructional advice - "aim a little to the left of the Object Ball's Center when using a Right Dominant Eye" - was too vague for a sport that requires constant precision. After all, how much is a 'little'? A 'little' will not mean the same amount to everyone.

So, I decided to give the aiming methods the same kind of scrupulous scrutinizing that I gave the Alignment elements. In order to leave no stone UN-turned; I dissected each one of the aiming methods that I was taught.

Once I set up my desired shot, I calculated the object balls required contact point to send it to the pocket. I began with the first method that I was taught - **The Imaginary Cue Ball** or **(Ghost Ball) Method**. I was told that many world class players use this method.

The Imaginary Cue Ball Method

The **Imaginary Cue Ball Method** says to imagine where the Cue Ball Center will be at the precise moment of impact when the cue ball hits the object ball's desired contact point. Then simply aim the **Cue Ball's Center** to that imaginary **Cue Ball's Center Point** on the tablecloth. The exact distance is 1 1/8 inch from the object ball contact point. (See below).

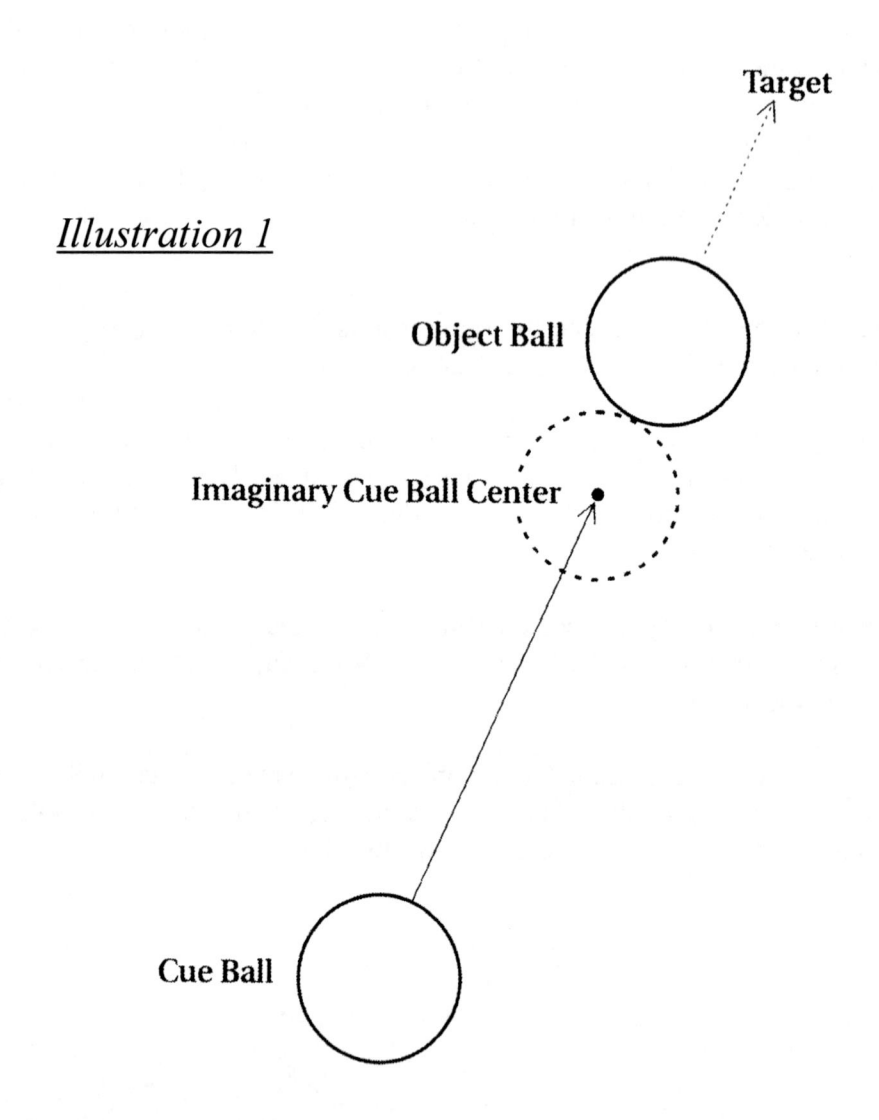

Illustration 1

Target

Object Ball

Imaginary Cue Ball Center

Cue Ball

See the following page and illustration for my personal evaluation regarding this method. (More on this Aim Method in the Applications chapter).

Many good pool players use the **Imaginary Cue Ball Method** with excellent results, but for me this method is only good for a limited range of shots.

This method was effective for me when the object ball was near a pocket and I didn't have to be concerned with precision when aiming, or with cue ball positioning afterwards. It is effective for me when I am shooting a straight shot and the cut shots which require less than a half-ball cut. However, when the *Imaginary* **Cue Ball Center Aim Point** exceeded the **Object Ball's Edge**.... My pocketing of balls became erratic. (See below).

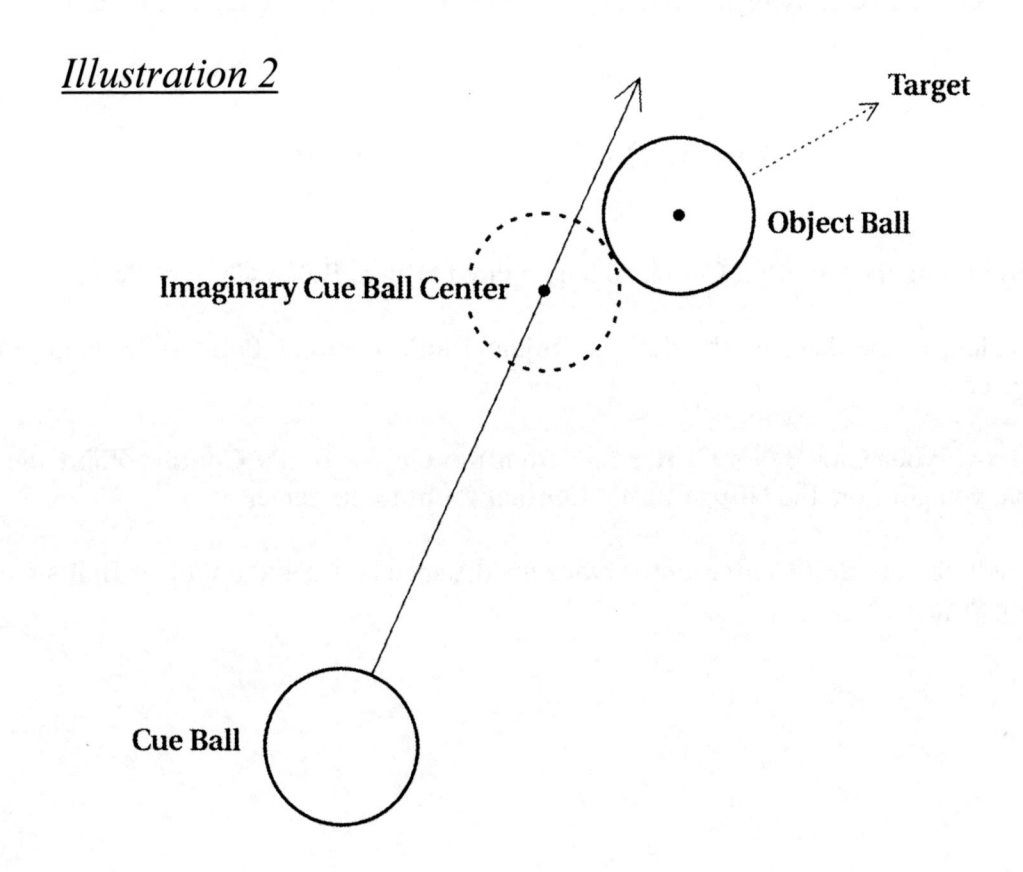

Illustration 2

The next aiming method that I carefully examined was - **The Double the Distance Method**. This is where you aim the **Cue Ball Center** to a point, which is the result of 'doubling the distance' from the **Object Ball's Center** and its contact point.

You should remember that the shape of the pool balls has a *'curving'* feature. An obvious, but overlooked feature is that the outline seems to bend from the Equator Edges to the top and bottom of the spherical object. This is an important characteristic to remember! One reason is that when you aim the center point on the **Equator Line** of a spherical cue ball to a particular point on a duplicate object ball (other than the center), contact will be made on the equator at a point halfway between the **Cue Ball** and **Object Ball's Center Points**.

In other words, the spherical pool balls will only touch their same equator center points when it's a straight shot. The **Cue Ball Equator Center Point** will not touch any other object point at the equator while shooting a regular cut shot. That's the basis for using **The Double-the-Distance Aim Method**. (By regular shot, I mean no masse`ing or jumping of the balls).

Double the Distance Method

Start by aiming the **Cue Ball Center** to the required **Object Ball's Contact Point**.

Then calculate the distance the desired **Object Ball's Contact Point** is from the **Object Ball's Center**.

Then move your **Cue Ball's Center** aim from the **Object Ball's Contact Point** the same amount that you got from the **Object Ball's Contact Point** to the center.

The resulting **Cue Ball Center** aim is twice the distance between the **Object Ball's Contact** and **Center Points**.

See illustrations 3 and 4.

Illustration 3

Target

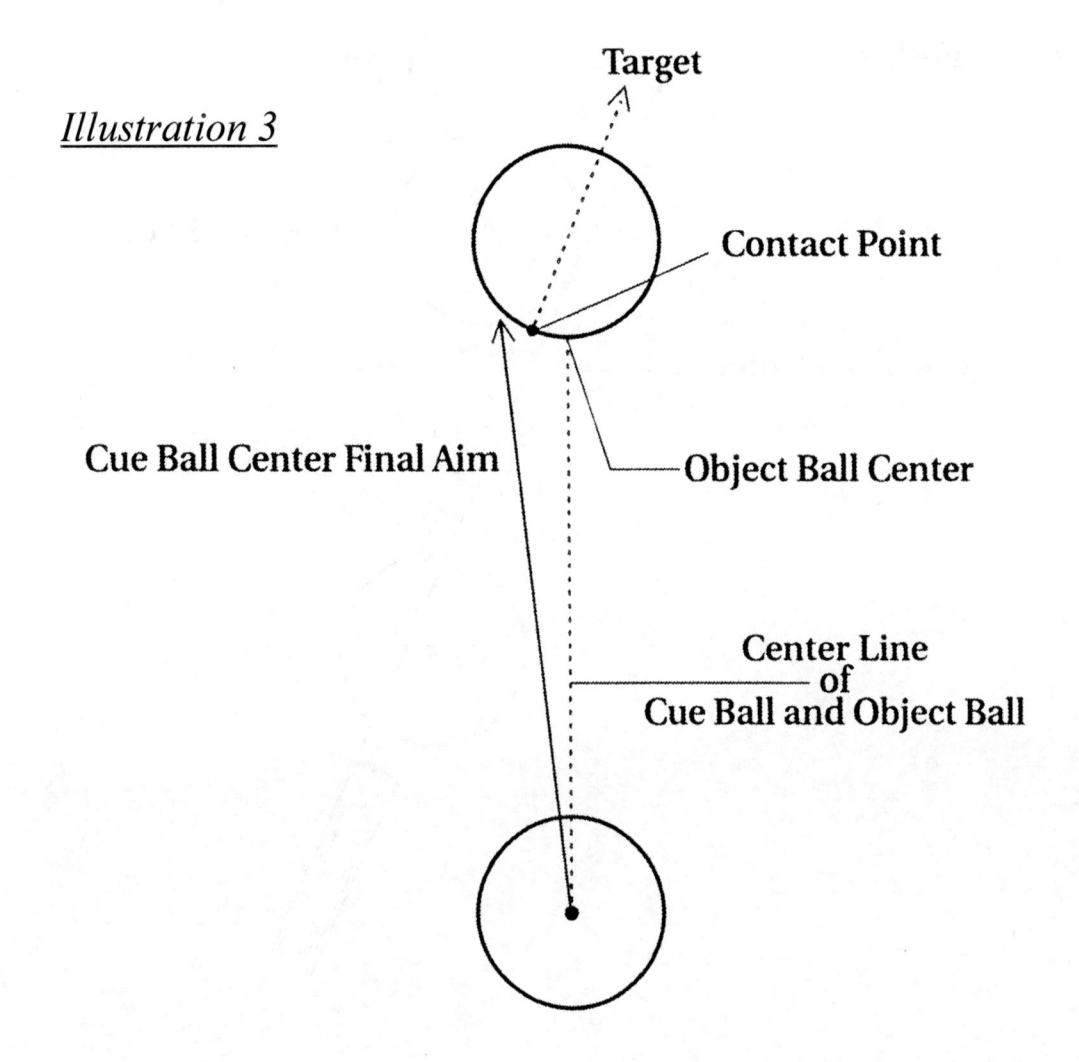

Contact Point

Cue Ball Center Final Aim

Object Ball Center

Center Line of Cue Ball and Object Ball

I find this method very difficult to use when the **Object Ball's Contact Point** is more than half-ball, because when I 'double the distance' as required, the aim of the **Cue Ball's Center** will be beyond the edge of the object ball. (You will then be aiming at air, or a tablecloth point, or a table cushion point which makes aiming more challenging).

The professional instruction given to me regarding the aiming beyond the **Object Ball's Edge** was to use cue-tip increments in relation to the **Object Ball's Edge**.

Illustration 4

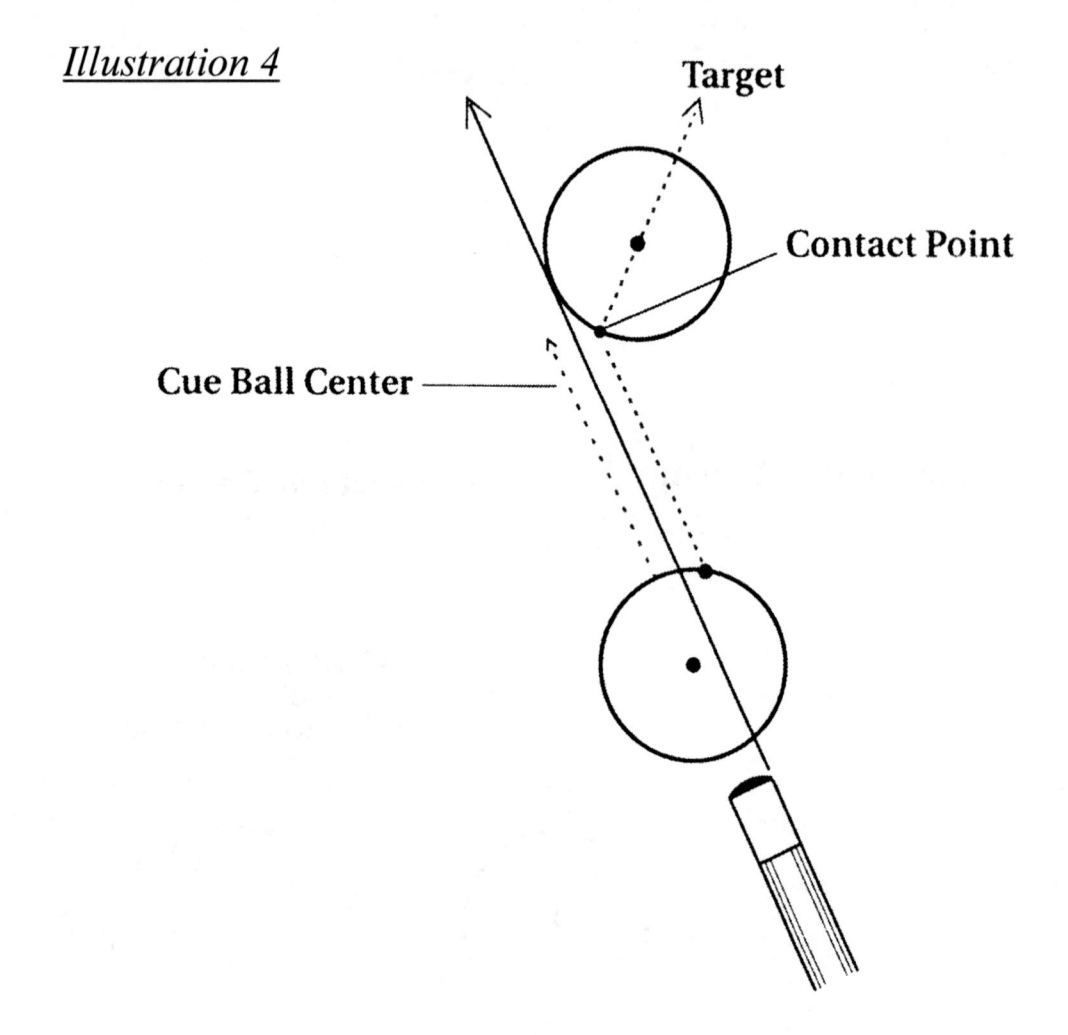

In the above illustration I am using a cue-tip increment by aiming the edge of my cue-tip to the **Object Ball's Edge**. Therefore, the **Cue Ball's Center** is pointed wider than the **Object Ball's Edge**. You are supposed to memorize that a specific object ball contact point will get a half cue-tip aim to **Object Ball's Edge**, or one and a half cue-tip aim, or two or three etc.

For one thing, I did not like the idea that I was required to memorize the specific cue-tip/object ball edge combinations for the various cut shots.

The last way that I was taught to aim is called - **The Contact to Contact Method**. This one is easy to explain. I've been told that most of the world class players and the overall better players use this method.

Contact to Contact Method

Simply aim the same contact point on the cue ball to the same **Object Ball's Contact Point**. I told you it was easy to explain. (See below).

Illustration 5

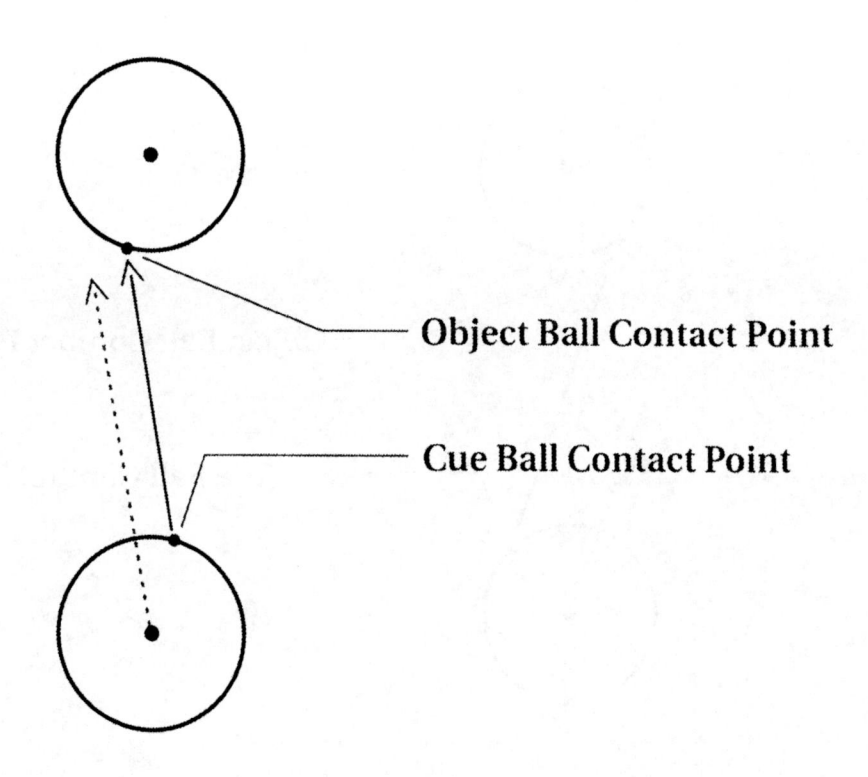

— Object Ball Contact Point

— Cue Ball Contact Point

See the following page and illustration for my personal evaluation regarding this method.

This method works best for me when the distance between the cue ball and object ball range from a couple of inches to a little less than about half a table length; also, when the cut is less than a half ball.

When I use the **Contact to Contact Method** for ¾ to full table length and for cut shots that are wider than a half ball.... My shooting percentage drops.

I can't use the **Contact to Contact Method** for the wider than half ball cut shots for a different reason than the **Imaginary** and **Double the Distance Methods**. It's because I find it awkward and difficult to align my face's **aiming focal point** directly over the cue ball's point when the point is wider than a half ball. I can not maintain a comfortable stance while I try to align my eye over the wide contact point and stroke the **Cue Ball's Center** in a straight line. (See below).

Illustration 6

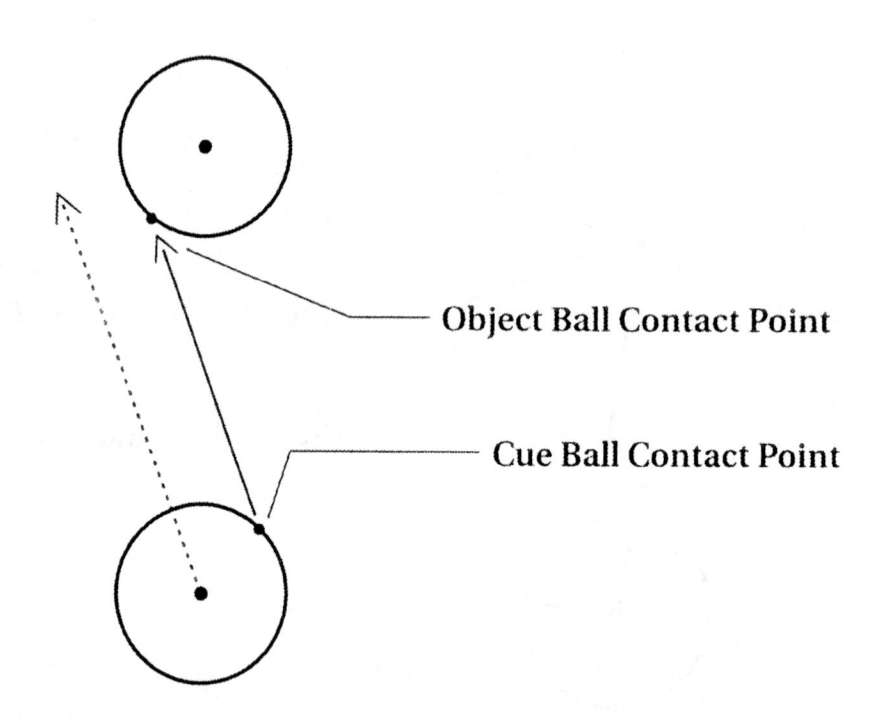

———— Object Ball Contact Point

———— Cue Ball Contact Point

Willie Mosconi.

I hate to say it, but for the longest time, I thought that some of the people whom I had asked (and paid) were not honest with me. I harbored that thought until I asked *Willie Mosconi*.

Willie said that he used the **Contact to Contact Method**. He made sure that he was set up properly behind the cue ball, before aiming and stroking the cue ball. Of course, when he demonstrated, *Willie* was able to feather the object ball with the cue ball, as well as, pocketing the long table shots with little trouble.

Although I was inspired by *Willie's* demonstration, I still had my same aiming inconsistencies. After seeing a thin cut shot made over and over, and the long shots consistently pocketed by the *Master Mosconi*, I was more convinced that 'something' from these aiming instructions had to be missing. So, I continued struggling with all three of these "*workable*" aiming methods for several years, while trying to create my own aiming method.

While I struggled, I wondered what could be missing from the aiming instructions. I realized that they couldn't all be dishonest with their explanations and instructions. And, I was not about to surrender my curiosity, because I firmly believed that I (and tens of millions of other pool players) have the same average intelligence and hand/eye coordination, as most of these better pool players.

I realized that even though the great players were able to exhibit greatness on the table, they couldn't always explain exactly what they were doing. Finally, I concluded that some of the better players and instructors were not consciously aware of aiming's minute details; they were probably 'consciously ignorant' of what they were doing instinctively.

This was driven home to me when I asked *Willie Mosconi* what he was thinking while he was running the racks on the night he ran 526 balls.

Willie told me that he was hardly doing any thinking while he was playing. He said he saw the patterns he needed to play and then just shot. He knew what to do as a result of all his years of practice. He said that he didn't worry about his aligning, or aiming, or stroking; he just did it. This told me that his playing was mostly instinctive. (Let me ask you: did you ever try to explain your instinctive behavior? It's like, uh.... It's not so easy. Is it?)

I remember one time when *Willie* was about to begin practicing after he didn't touch his cue for a long time. He told me that he was concerned about remembering "how to hit 'em". When I asked *Willie* to elaborate he said he needed to explain on the pool table rather than talk about it. He just pointed out the **Cue Ball's Contact Point** that he was going to aim to the required **Object Ball's Contact Point**, and then shot.

He continued his visual explanations for several shots. That was it! He said that he didn't know how to explain it any further. His years of hard practice and the competitive playing against top-notched rivals had lifted his skills to another level.

Do you think that, maybe, when some of the great players reach their "great level of play", there is no reason for them to bog their minds down by trying to explain what they have already mastered?

And how about some of the players, who know that they could explain their techniques on a more comprehensive level, but won't teach? Perhaps, because of the high-caliber competition they face while earning their livelihood and the possible future showdowns with the young aspiring players, the disclosing of their "secrets" would, eventually, prove to be detrimental to them.

Eventually, I was able to learn that, even though I had studied with great and not- so-great teachers, they all had something to offer.

As the years slowly passed, I realized how much easier it is to criticize an aiming method than to create one. But I persevered. (Yes, with my experimenting and criticizing).

Pool Eyes

The way I see it, now, it was necessary for me to find new ways to accomplish what I was after. And finding the new ways ultimately meant finding new ways of "pool thinking". At the same time that I resigned my laborious efforts, in looking for those mysterious and privileged pool secrets with the way I was taught, I began uncovering some surprising truths. ***Truths that were not mysterious or clandestine, but, rather subtle and simply overlooked.***

Instituting new pool terms such as; the "**Facial Guide Points**", and the "**Real Equator Line**" has greatly helped to better my Pool mentality. They had become my allies in my battle against *Pool Ignorance* and assisted me in locating some of my *invisible pool enemies*.

However, it wasn't until I did more research and experimented with different approaches that I, finally, began to see some light at the end of the tunnel. New phrases like; "**Outward-Inward Eye Sight Angles**", the "**Real Cue-ball Center Aim Point**" and the "**Back Cue-ball Center Point**", and "**Eye-Switching**" helped to broaden my understanding, even more. Also, as you will learn, the word "*Apparent*" led me to more ways for recognizing and correcting my pool faults and it proves to be an invaluable word in my pool vocabulary.

I will try to show you that the process of aiming spherical-shaped balls involves more than meets the normal *untrained* eye. In order to succeed with consistent execution, whether it be in playing the various Pool games, Billiard games, Snooker (and I'll even throw in Bumper Pool), you must develop what I like to call.... "**Pool Eyes**".

Pool Eyes help you to recognize the various nuances concerning the games that I have just mentioned. They can see more than the lesser-trained eyes. I'm not saying that if your vision is not 20-20 and you need eyeglasses to play, you do not already have, or will get **Pool Eyes**. Not at all! Because the **Pool Eyes** that I'm referring to are *insightful.* They dwell in our "**Pool Minds**".

Oh, yes! The process of aiming in these games requires some very sensitive skills, indeed. Even, if you were lucky enough to be born with some or all of these prerequisites, to develop these skills, you must study carefully and use efficient practice time at the table.

I'll let you in on a secret, if your improvement has reached a stagnant point for longer than you think it should be lasting, and you just feel inside or know that you can play better, remember this saying: "*If you keep doing what you're doing, you'll keep getting what you're getting*". Simply translated - "**Try doing it another way**". (And, while you're at it, why not take a lesson?)

AHEAD

There are

New Phrases

And

New Thoughts!

Straight Shooting Test

Please Note: The **purpose of the following exercises is to test your (*straight*) Aim and Stroke!** It will best serve you when done on a well-lit pool table that is clean and level.

I think it is best to start the straight-shooting test with only the cue ball. Let's begin with an old teaching exercise, which has you; place the cue ball on one of the table's spots. (By the way, I was told that this is an old hustler's trick. You'll see what I mean in a few pages). I'm going to ask you to shoot the cue ball on an imaginary straight line to the center of the table's diamond on the short rail. Because the diamond in the rail is flat, it will probably be hard to see when in your shooting position. So, it will help you to substitute your mark by placing an object directly over the center of the diamond, or you can mark (wet or chalk) the front of the rail as your aim point.

Go ahead and aim the cue ball at the mark and disregard the other table spot, because the table spot might not be located precisely on a straight line to the exact center of the table's diamond. You will be stroking the cue ball 'center ball' (without a trace of cue ball English), because you will be trying to have the cue ball roll straight back over the same spot after hitting the rail.

See the following illustration.

Illustration 7

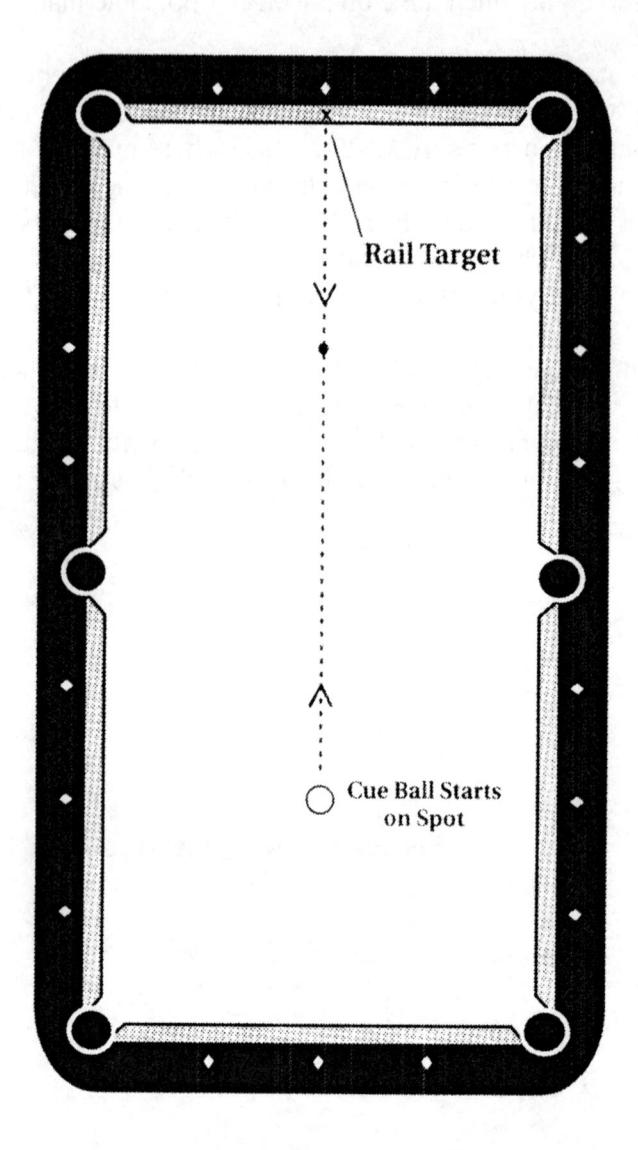

How did you do? Did the cue ball at least rebound near the table spot? Do this at least 10 times before going to the next example.

Now, place the cue ball exactly one diamond to any side of the table spot. It can be to the right side of the table spot or to the left. And then center your object (Aim mark) over the first diamond from the short rail's center table diamond. It will be the same side of the table's center diamond as you have placed the cue ball.

Repeat the previous exercise by striving to have the cue ball roll straight back over the 1 diamond spot on the table after hitting the rail. (See below).

Illustration 8

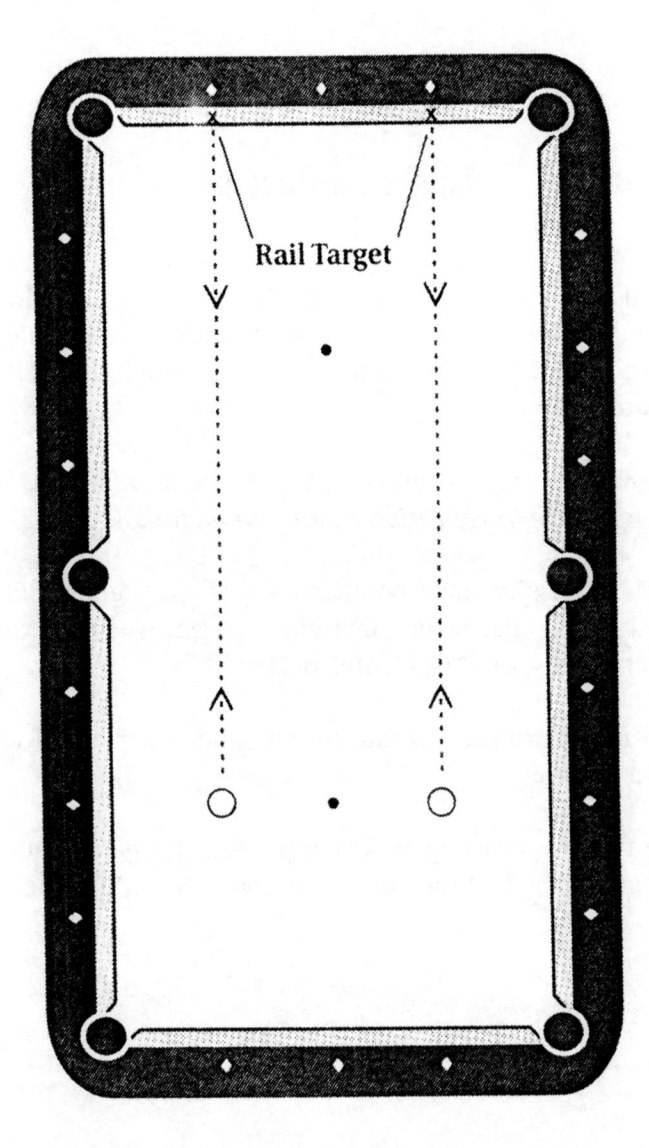

How did you do this time? How many times out of ten did you roll the cue ball over the mark? Did you do worse than the first one?

15

Were you successful the both times?

If you were not successful both times, were you more successful the first time? Do you know why you were better the first time?

And of course, if you were not successful both times, *do you know how to correct what you were doing wrong?* I ask this, because there are countless times when after you correct some people's mistakes, they will tell you.... "Oh! I knew that! I'm just not warmed up yet". So, to you people, I say, "Go warm up and try it again".

Okay, if you were successful with the first exercise and not the second, do you think that (maybe) it was because the table light over the pool table helped you select the **Cue Ball Center Point?**

Light Reflection

How? Go back and set up the cue ball over the table spot and look at the table light's reflection on the ball. If the table lights are properly set, they will be centered over the table spot and the reflection will be centered over the cue ball. Thus, the light's reflection will be directly over the **Cue Ball's Center.**

Let me state now, that I am only using the light reflection to help make a point! I am not, or will not advocate using the light reflection as an aim method.

So, if you were not successful, take another look at the light reflection and try the first exercise again. Did you have better results this time? If so, was it because (maybe) you were able to judge the location of the **Cue Ball Center better?**

Now try this. Use a marker to draw a thin line around the cue ball and make sure that the whole line is straight and centered.

Go back and do the two exercises again, using the drawn line as your substitute for the cue ball center. (Keep this line on the ball for future reference. See Illustration 9).

Set up the cue ball so that the line represents the **Cue ball's Center Point**. The line should be vertical with the table spot. (See below).

Illustration 9

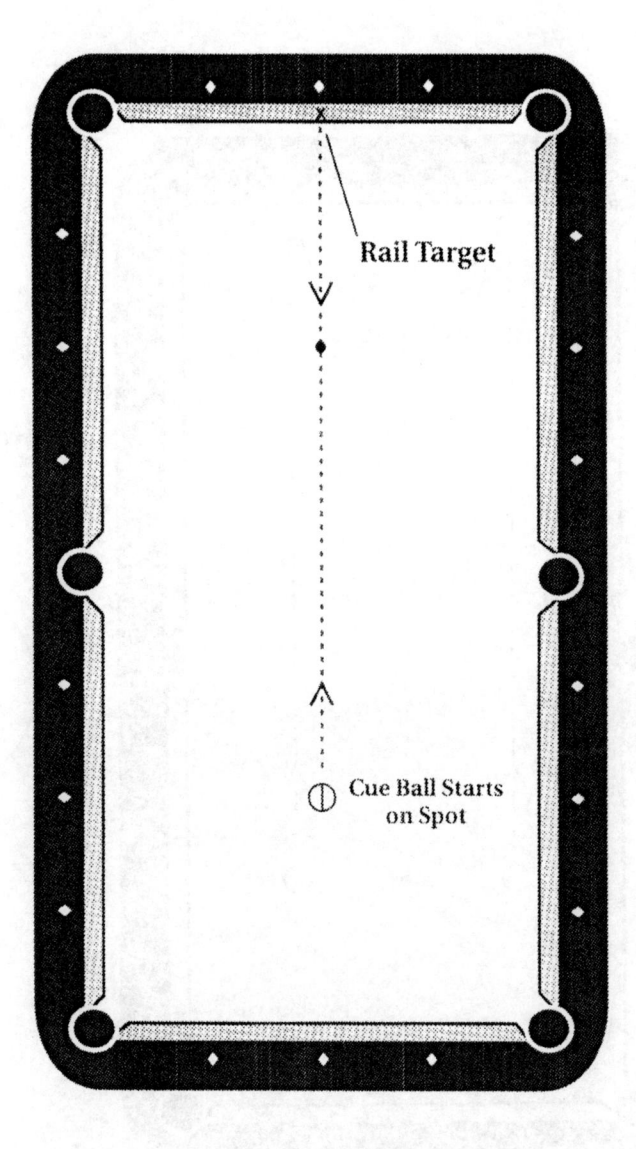

Take notice of where the light reflection is compared to the line in the middle of the ball. With the cue ball on the spot, you should see that the light reflection is exactly over the line.

If the light reflection is not centered over the line that you've drawn, and you have turned the line to be vertical with the table, then the light fixture is not set up appropriately. I recommend you move to a suitable table.

Now, before you attempt the second exercise again, take a look at the light reflection on the ball, as the cue ball is sitting one diamond to the side of the table spot. (See below).

Off-Centered Light Reflection

Illustration 10

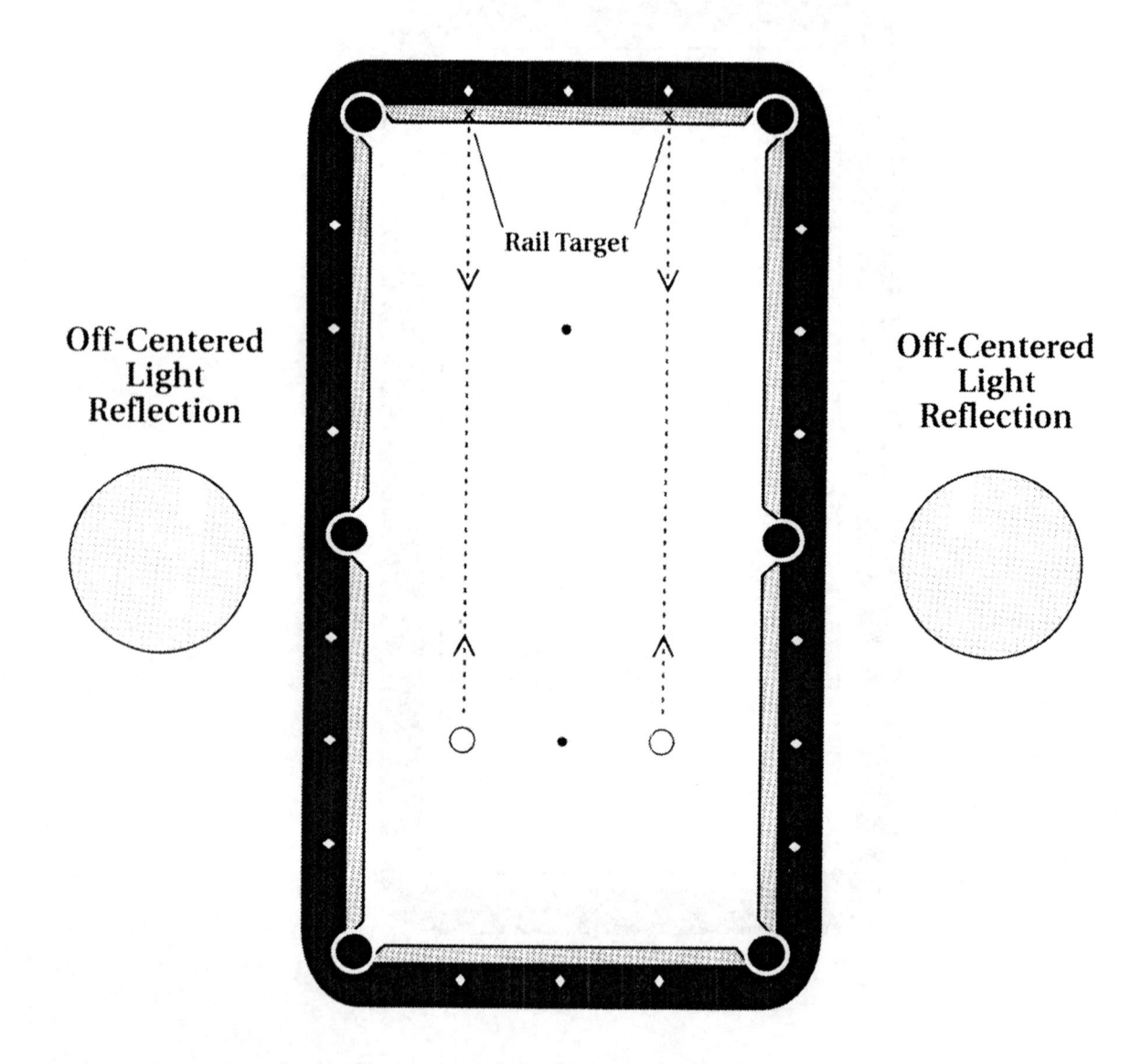

Even if you're trying this on a bar table, you should notice that the light reflection is off-centered. (If not, move to another table or come back and try it when you're not "feeling so good". You sober minded people know what I mean).

Did it help your aiming by knowing that the reflection was not centered in this second example?

*Let me say again, that I am not, nor will I be advocating the using of the table's light reflection as part of an aiming method. *I do not advocate aiming at any "light point" on the object ball that is not on the Real Equator*. As you will notice, all the light reflections appear <u>above</u> the point where the cue ball and object ball will make contact. Because of the various "looks" that the reflections will show on the cue ball and object ball at the various positions, there are too many compensations that have to be considered. **DO YOURSELF A BIG FAVOR AND FORGET ABOUT THE LIGHT REFLECTIONS!** In this chapter, I am only using the light reflection on the ball in this exercise as a visual aid to identify the **Cue Ball Center.**

So, if you think that you've been using the **Cue Ball Center Point** that is on the **Real Equator** and you are still having a difficult time shooting the cue ball straight (with the proper stroke), then I have something that will definitely help you.

What could it be? No! Don't worry! There are no fancy or expensive aiming gizmos to buy. What I have to show you is free and simple to do. Okay, I'll give you a hint - *You are not completely centering your aim and/or stroke over the shot.*

And what I am about to show you in the following chapters have been in front of my face and your face all along, and especially, the *cue ball's face*. I think, that after you read the **Aiming the Cue Ball** and **The Real Cue Ball Center Aim Point** Chapters, you will change the way that you look at the cue ball *forever*.

ALIGNMENT

In my opinion, one of the most crucial factors in pool is Alignment. But, almost all of the beginners and advanced players that I talked to were not aware of it.

Without proper knowledge of the alignment between the player's body and the aim line through the cue ball, the players' execution skills will suffer. So, I strongly advise that the reader becomes very familiar with this Alignment's orientation chapter before going ahead to the aiming chapters.

Remember: The purpose of this chapter is to acquaint you with some important Alignment elements and knowledge, knowledge that will enhance your perception of your aiming and your stroking.

By alignment, I mean the arranging of the shooter's body, head and eyes in relation to the aim line and cue ball when aiming the cue ball to hit a target. The target can be an object ball or a rail point.

It is also very important to know the proper location of the cue stick to the shooter's face, body and aim line, because *the cue stick is used as a reference tool while aiming and aligning.*

Peripheral Sighting

The cue stick helps in calculating our *direction of aim* from our body through the cue ball to our target, even, if it is only used with our **peripheral sighting**. Thus, if you have an incorrect cue/face alignment, your aiming is effected. (By peripheral-sighting, I mean seeing outside or inside your straight line of focus. See examples in The Aiming The Cue Ball chapter).

Focal Point

When I look at an object, I used to think of my nose as always on a straight line to the center of that object. I innately thought that my nose was always, my face's precise **Focal Point**. (**Focal Points** are the ones directly over the aim line). Later, I was forced to find myself guilty of not giving this the proper amount of thought. (See the following illustration).

Illustration 11

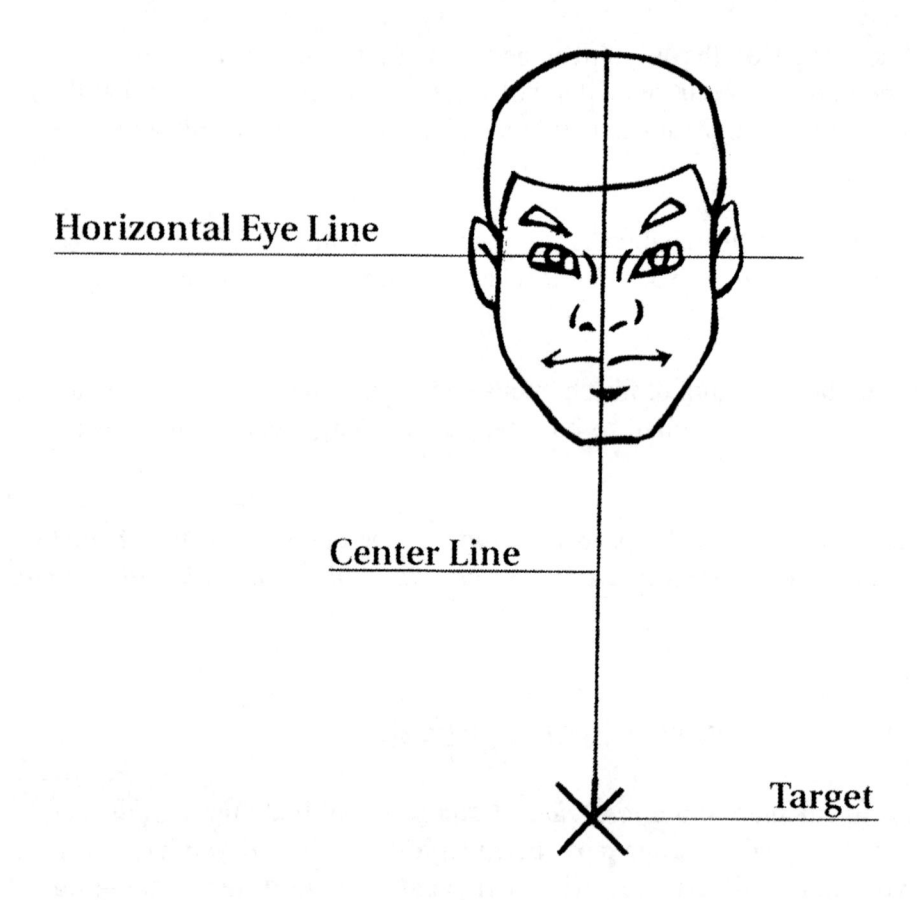

[Diagram of a face with Horizontal Eye Line across the eyes, Center Line running vertically down through the nose and jaw to a Target marked with an X below]

Equi-angled and Equidistant Eyes

Note: I call this alignment *The Nose Center Alignment.* The **Nose** and **Jaw Center Points** are the **Focal Point**s in this example. The Eyes are both even with the **Horizontal Line** which means there is no head tilt. Both eyes are **equi-angled and equidistant** from the **Nose's Centerline** and aim line. Thus, there is no **Dominant Eye** or a **Pure Eye**.

The object of focus is located on an imaginary straight line to the center of the nose. The *head is straight* which allows all of the **Nose's Centerline** and the center of the jaw to be directly over the aim line.

Straight Head

I think that Aiming straight is best learned and executed when based on having a Straight Head. By "Straight Head", I mean that the Nose Centerline and the Chin Center are **vertically lined up** with the Cue Ball and the Object Ball's Contact Point. (No side way tilting of the head!).

However, in alignment, I stumbled on a very important subtlety with enormous value; without realizing it, we are constantly *turning* and *tilting* our body and head while our eyes automatically adjust. So, even if the tilting or turning is very slight, *our eye's distance to the Nose Centerline will not be evenly spaced, nor their straight lines of sight equally angled*.

So, what does this have to do with shooting pool? It has everything to do with it.

This nuance has a direct effect on our *aim perception* and the *perception of our body's positioning* with the cue stick and the balls that we are aiming. The more your head is tilted, or turned off-centered from the imaginary aim line, the more off-angled your eyes will be looking at the object. This is because they will automatically compensate for this tilting and turning. And, since this compensating is done without our usual awareness, our perception of the shot will probably be wrong, because, without trained eyes, we will be instinctively basing our aim on having equidistant and equi-angled eyes.

Why is this important to understand? Most of you are probably instinctively basing your aim perception on having your alignment straight with the center of the object. But at the same time, only thinking you are aiming with a straight (vertically) head using either a Pure Eye, or Two Evenly Spaced Eyes that are evenly-angled. (See the Aim Starting Point in Aiming The Cue Ball chapter).

Study the following three illustrations that will demonstrate what may happen (unintentionally) to a shooter's intended Nose Center Alignment with his Two Evenly Focused Eyes.

Turned Head

Now, let's see what happens to our eyes in relation to the **Nose Centerline** and the imaginary aim line when we turn and tilt our heads.

Illustration 12

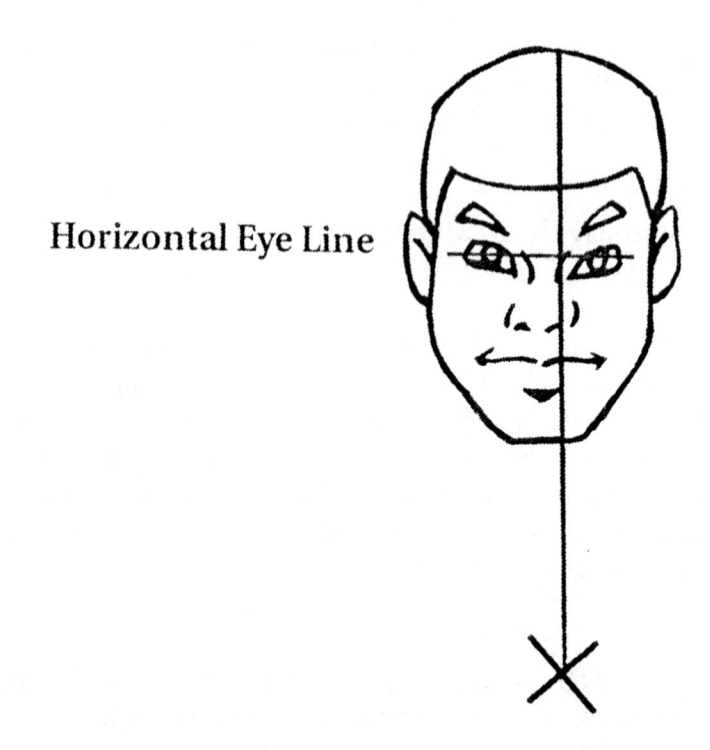

Horizontal Eye Line

Note: The player's eyes are not equidistant or equi-angled with the aim line however, they are even with the **Straight Head's Horizontal Eye Line**. The head is *turned* to the player's right side. As a result, the player's left eye is a little closer to the **Nose's Centerline**. The **Nose's Centerline** and **Jaw Center Point** *parallel* the sketched vertical aim line, hence, they are not straight over it. Thus, there is a great chance that the player is <u>unintentionally</u> using the left or right eye, as a **Dominant Eye** or a **Pure Eye**.

The head is turned and the eyes have automatically adjusted for this turning. Now, look at where the sketched line is intersecting the face. It's <u>not</u> the **Nose** and **Jaw Center Points**!

Tilted Head

Illustration 13

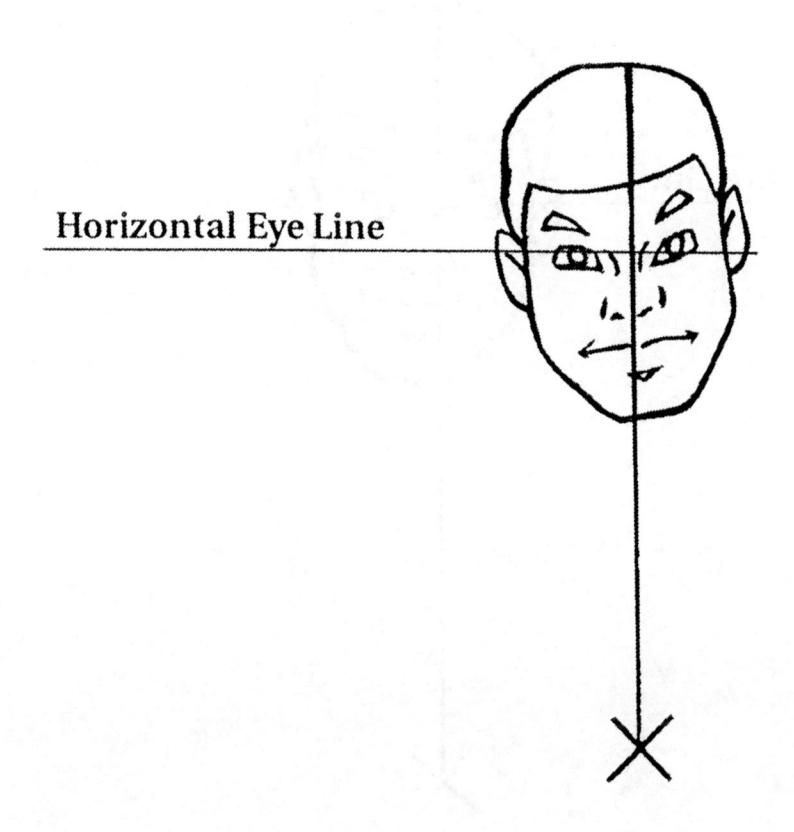

Horizontal Eye Line

Note: The eyes are *off-centered* from the **Straight Head's Horizontal Eye Line**. Here the player's right eye is a little lower than his left eye. The **Jaw Center Point** and the **Nose Centerline** *crosses over* the imaginary aim line. Either the left or right eye of the shooter might be used, <u>unintentionally,</u> as a **Dominant Eye** or a **Pure Eye**.

In this example, it is hard to get an accurate perception of the aim line, because the head is *tilted* to the right.

Turned and Tilted Head

Illustration 14

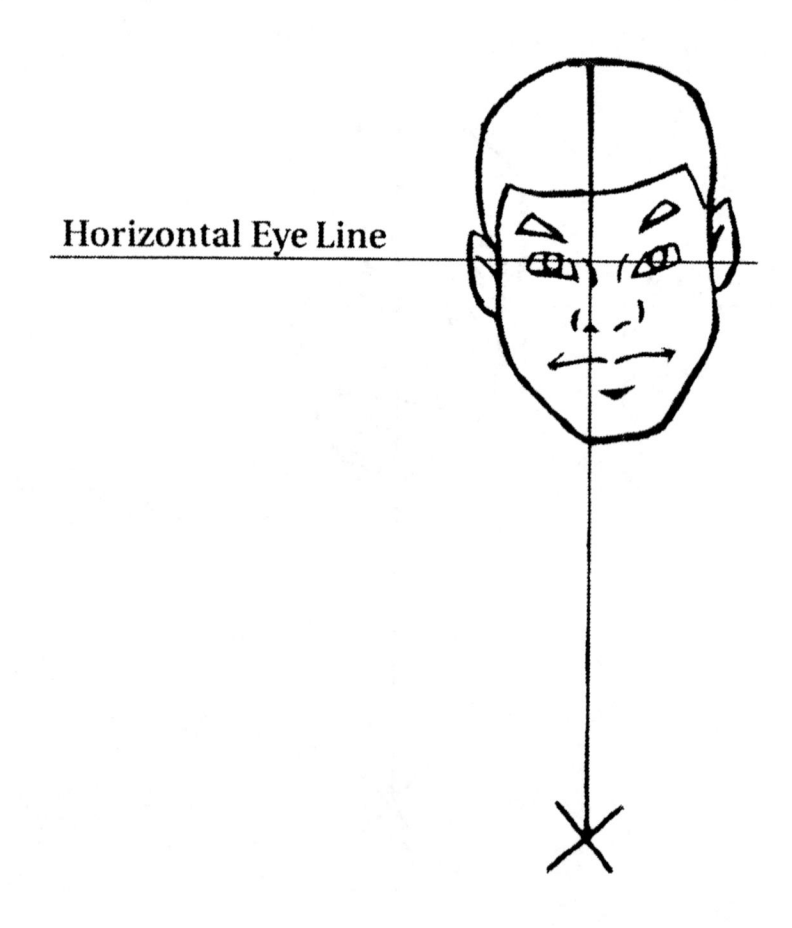

Note: The **Nose Centerline** and the **Jaw's Center Point** does not intersect the imaginary aim line at any point and both eyes are not on the **Straight Head's Horizontal Eye Line**. The left eye is higher than the right eye. The eyes are not equidistant from the aim line. Again, either the left or right eye might be used, <u>unintentionally</u>, as a **Dominant Eye** or a **Pure Eye**.

It is even harder to accurately judge the aim line with this type of alignment, because the player's head is ***turned and tilted*** to the right.

Why am I showing you the sketched aim line to the center of the object, the **Nose's Centerline**, the turned and tilted head, equidistant eyes etc.?

They are meant as an introduction, to those of you who are innocently ignorant of their existence, to make your familiarizing of these *imaginary* and *subtle* elements easier and, because I refer to the **Nose Centerline Alignment** with two evenly-spaced and evenly-angled eyes in the later chapters. Therefore, I strongly advocate that all pool players acquaint themselves with these basic principles, even, if they do not use their **Nose Centerline.**

Just as the majority of people would **assume** that their **Nose Centerline** is always centered to the object of their focus, nearly all the amateur and advanced players assume that they are aligning their cue stick with the center of their jaw and nose. While attempting to aim with Two Evenly-Spaced Eyes and a straight head ***they will seldom align themselves the way that they think***, because of their instinctive body twisting and turning into comfortable shooting positions. And, therefore, their perception of the cue ball and object ball's aim line will be wrong.

Even though, the majority of the players I've talked to thought they were positively centering directly over the aim line, they had their heads slightly turned and/or tilted. And, since, they use their cue stick as an aiming tool.... Their aim and stroke was off. So, how could they actually expect to consistently aim and stroke straight to any target?

If you don't know your personal **Facial Focal Points** (Face's precise alignment over the aim line), try this illustration at home or the poolroom.

Mirror Aid

Get a mirror (at least the size of this page), a 4-6 inch long string, two strips of tape, a cue ball or object ball, your cue stick and the aid of a friend. A friend will help you locate your true alignment with their objective view.

Set the mirror on a flat surface and angle it so that you'll be able to see your face and cue ball when you simulate your normal and comfortable shooting position. (Try to have the mirror the same height above the floor as a pool table). Tape the top and bottom of the string in a vertical line on the center of the mirror. Now, center the cue ball in front of the mirror a few inches from the string. (See below).

Illustration 15

28

Then, with your cue stick in hand, approach the cue ball (and string), as you normally would do when shooting a shot, and bend down into your normal shooting position. (The string represents the imaginary aim line. The 'reflected' cue ball represents an object ball).

Place your bridge hand the same distance from the cue ball as you normally do. Make sure that your head is lowered the same distance as when you are shooting over your shots. Once you are set - **FREEZE YOUR WHOLE BODY!** (See below).

Illustration 16

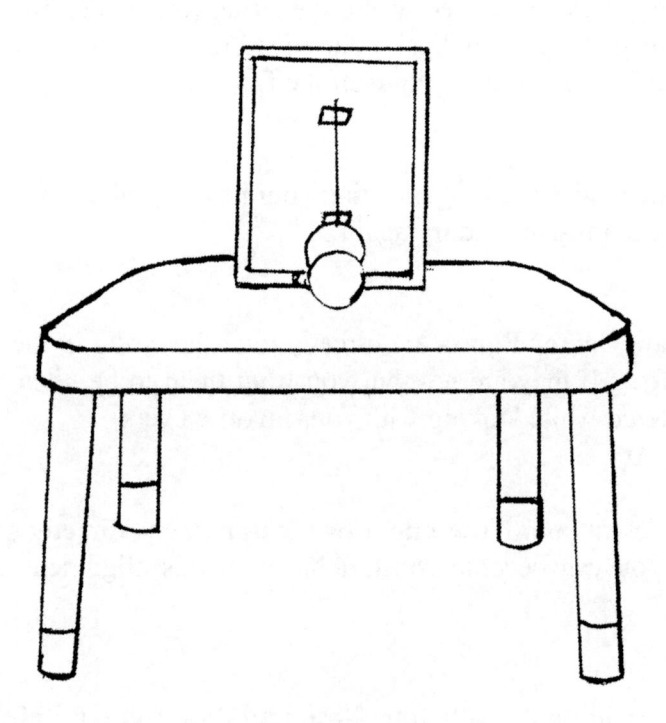

Without moving your head or body, look at where the string is in relation to your face and cue stick. Is it where you thought it would be?

Now, **continue to freeze,** and look at the string with your different eye(s). By this, I mean squint and use only your right eye (Right Pure Eye). Do the same with your left eye. Of course, try to look with Two Evenly Focused Eyes. (For me to get my two eyes evenly-focused, I need about two seconds to actually focus my eyes on the object when I am playing regularly. I need several seconds when I begin to play after a layoff. My point is that it takes more time for me to evenly-focus my two eyes on an object than with my **Pure Eye!**)

I'm sure you noticed that the string *seems* to intersect different places on your face when you look at it with different eye positions while keeping your head still.

Which is your natural and favorite way to aim? Is it **Right Pure Eye?** Is it Two Evenly Focused Eyes? Is it with the **Left Dominant Eye etc.**?

With your favorite eye(s), can you see where the string (imaginary aim line) intersects your face in the mirror? Actually, you should ask your friend to verify your face's precise locations, because it can be difficult to judge this by yourself the first time.

Can you tell if you are slightly turning or tilting your head? Take time to see if you are tense anywhere, if so, relax those muscles and try again.

If your **Nose and Jaw Center Points** are directly over the string in the mirror then they are <u>your</u> **Facial Focal Point**s. If they are not, but you want them to be, then move your head and body, until they are centered while looking with your favorite eye(s).

Are you comfortable with your **Nose and Jaw Center** Points directly over the aim line? If not, do you think that you can become comfortable with this alignment after some time and practice?

*If you can not get comfortable with your **Nose and Jaw Center Points** over the aim line then don't worry. I will address aligning and aiming with other face/cue alignments in a later chapter. But for now, please continue reading this chapter.

If you did not already, look now at where the cue stick intersects your face at the eyebrow, teeth, nose, shoulder and upper body parts, as well. ***Remember to look at these points with your favorite eye(s), because, as you have already seen, you will see slightly different facial and body alignment parts when looking with different eye positions.**

Now, I will show you how to use your facial and body alignment parts to help you get consistent aiming and stroking.

The **Eyebrow Point** or **Upper Nose Area** will serve as your *Upper Alignment Guide Point*. Take note of the precise location. Is it the middle or to the left a little, etc.?

Your particular **Top Tooth** and/or **Nose Point** will serve as your *Middle Alignment Guide Point*. Is it the middle of the top left tooth, or edge of the second etc? Does it intersect the middle or edge of your nose? The **Middle Alignment Point** aligns with the area just below the cue ball and around the upper shaft of your cue stick.

The **Chin Point** will serve as your *Bottom Alignment Guide Point*. Here is where you can watch the cue-butt area as you are stroking. You will be able to better see if you are stroking straight, or on an angle.

*Remember to look through each of your personal guide points with your same favorite eye(s)!

Guide Points

Ask your friend to verify your alignment and aim perception while you are ready to shoot a shot. Ask your friend to coach your movement as you search for the correct aim to the target. You can make any adjustments in front of the mirror and commit the corrections to memory. Note how just a slight movement will affect your perception of your alignment with the aim line. Then you can reciprocate by helping your friend with their **Guide Points.**

(In regards to your pool buddy who is helping you out with your alignment; We all know that Paybacks are a !#Ö%&$%%, but be honest when you help them with their alignment and **Guide Points.** Consequently, what goes around comes around. Besides, their improvement will help you to improve, too).

Remember that the **Focal Point**s on your face are the ones directly over the aim line. However, W.C. Fields cue sticks do not apply.

When you are satisfied, ***take a mental photograph of where your personal facial alignment points are precisely located.*** I can not over stress the importance of knowing your **Guide Points** in regards to shooting consistently. My shooting problems were due to lack of this knowledge. As a direct result from me learning about the **Guide Points**, it was much easier for me to change my alignment to suit my needs.

The purpose of showing you the mirror demonstration is to help you improve your judgment of your face/cue alignment while looking over the aim line. I hope that you will find improvement and satisfaction with it the way that I have. It helped the visualizing of my alignment a great deal.

By the way, take a look at the different alignments of the male and female professional players. See who uses your style and let them know about it. Maybe, they can offer you some more advice.

Footing in Alignment

You will find that the *initial placement* of your **Back Foot** (my right foot) during your *initial shooting stance* is more important than you thought. Before you bend over the cue ball to shoot, your **Back Foot's** alignment with the extended aim line on the floor will aid the rest of your body and head in aligning comfortably over the cue ball and aim line. (Left-handers will, of course, use their left foot).

You might be surprised to learn that just a slight change of your **Back Foot's** *initial position* to the floor's extended aim line will affect your body's (waist and chest) bending over, as well as, your feet's pivoting into final position.

As a way to get started, compare your **initial Back Foot's placement** with the following examples. See what specific **Foot Point** aligns you to your favorite facial alignment points. Experiment with pivoting your feet before you bend over to shoot. Closely monitor the way your body actually bends over the shot.

Do you go straight down without twisting your body?

Do you turn your waist as you bend? Is all your bending before or during your descent?

Do you bend both your knees? If so, how much? Do you bend them before or during your descent?

Are you relaxed as you bend down? Are you needlessly holding your breath?

Eliminate all unnecessary turning and twisting! Simplify your process of bending over the shot. The less you do; the easier it is to remember. **But don't sacrifice movement for comfort!**

Illustration 17

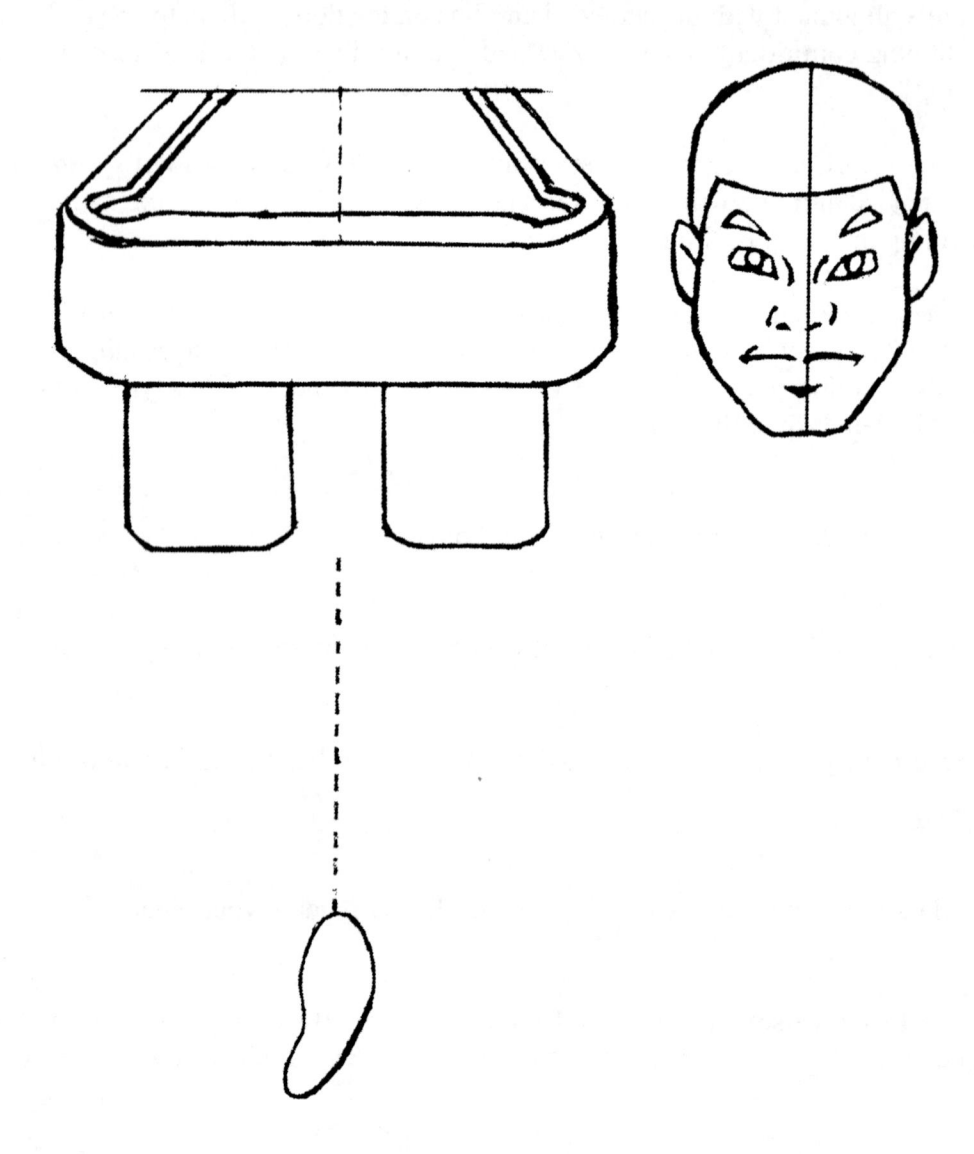

Big Toe

Note: Addressing the extended floor aim line with the center of my ***right big toe*** and <u>then pivoting my right foot</u>, before I bend over the shot, will help to ***naturally*** align my **Nose Centerline** over the aim line through the **Cue Ball Center**.

By naturally, I mean without the extra turning of your body. By slight pivoting, I mean turning the right foot to about 30°-40° with the floor's extended aim line without lifting it from the original spot.

Illustration 18

Left Eye Point

— The floor's extended Aim Line

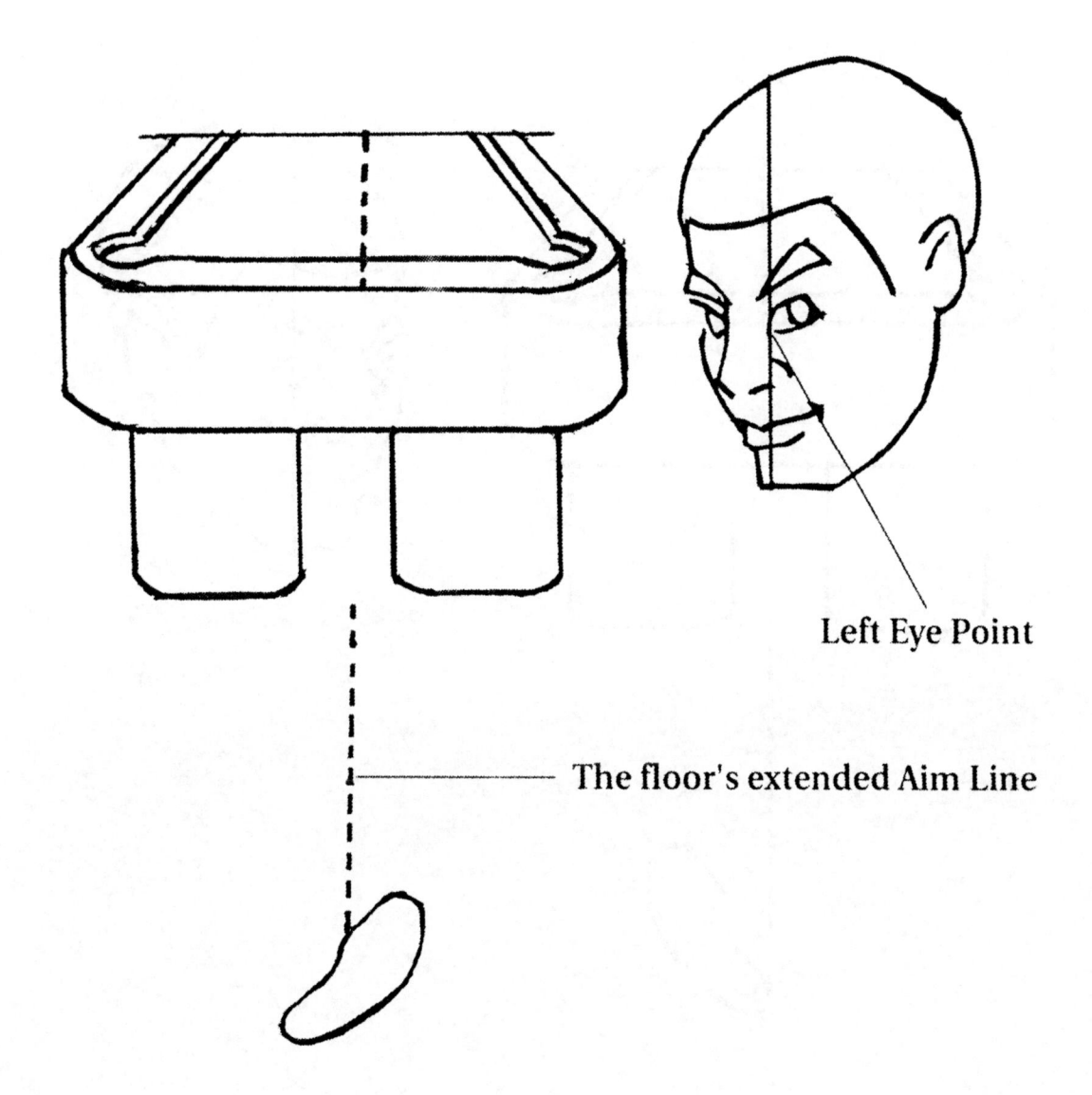

Left Eye Point

Note: The shooter starts by placing the **instep of his right foot** next to the extended aim line <u>before he starts his pivoting</u>. It helps him to align naturally to a point between his left eye and **Nose Centerline** over the aim line.

*I call this facial point the **Left Eye Point.**

Illustration 19

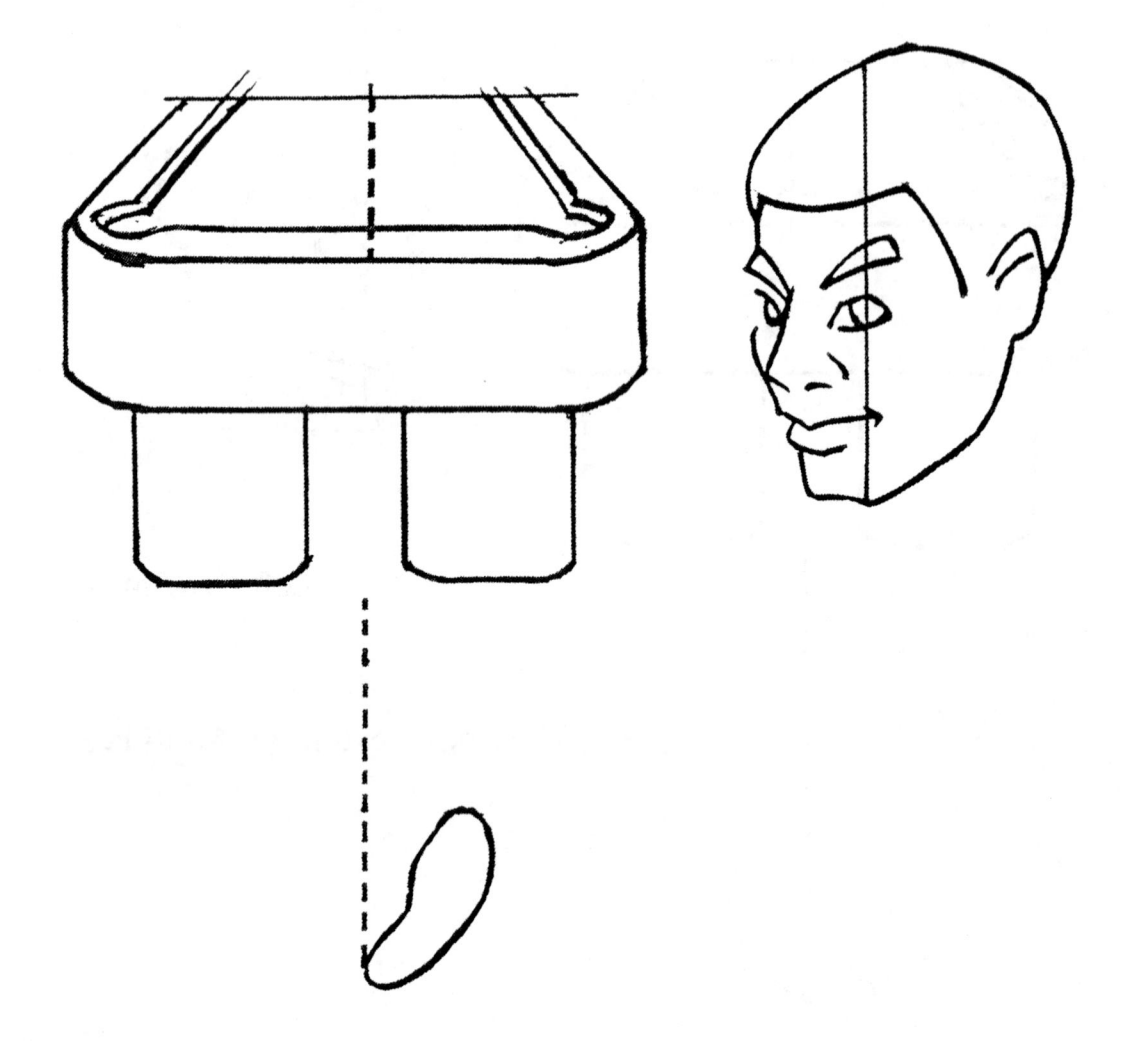

Pure Eye Aim

Note: Here the shooter starts with the ***back of his right heel*** to the floor's extended aim line and <u>then pivots</u> until his **Left Eye's Center** (Pure Left Eye) is directly over the aim line.

I call this **Pure Eye** over the aim line the *Rifle-Shooting Alignment.*

Illustration 20

Right Eye Point

Back of heel after pivoting

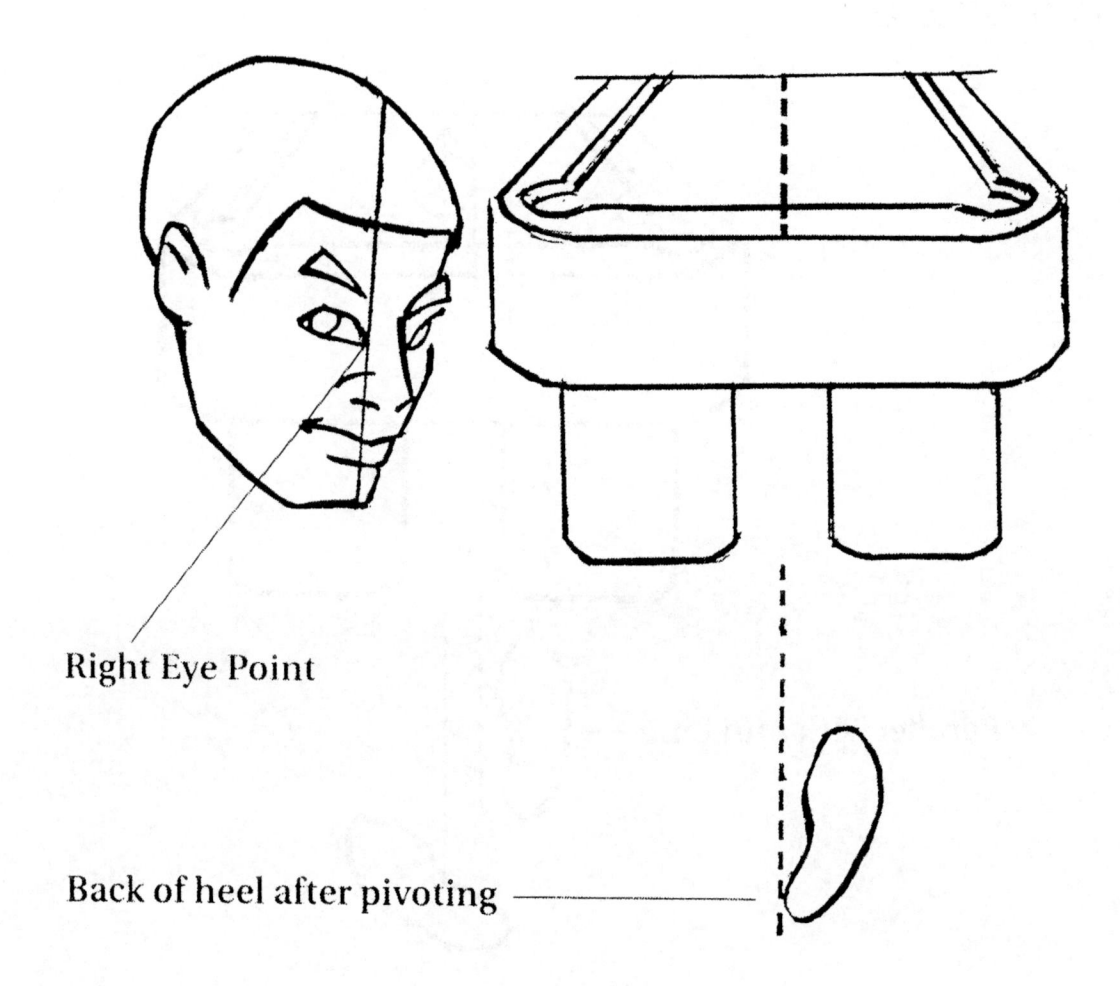

Right Eye Point

Note: The initial placement with the *center* of the shooter's *right foot's second toe*, before he bends over the shot, leaves him aligning his **Right Eye Point** over the aim line.

Note Well: In the shooter's *final* position after pivoting on his back heel, his back heel is aligned with aim line.

Please remember to spend time with your **Front Foot** because there is a very important relationship between the final placement of the **Front Foot** and the process of aligning the head.

For one thing, the parallel aim of the **Front Foot** helps keeps the turning of the waist in check while pivoting the body and the **Back Foot**. Another good thing about *paralleling* the **Front Foot** is that it is very accommodating serving as a guide, while trying to maintain a Straight Head Alignment every time you bend over the shot. (See the illustration below).

Illustration 21

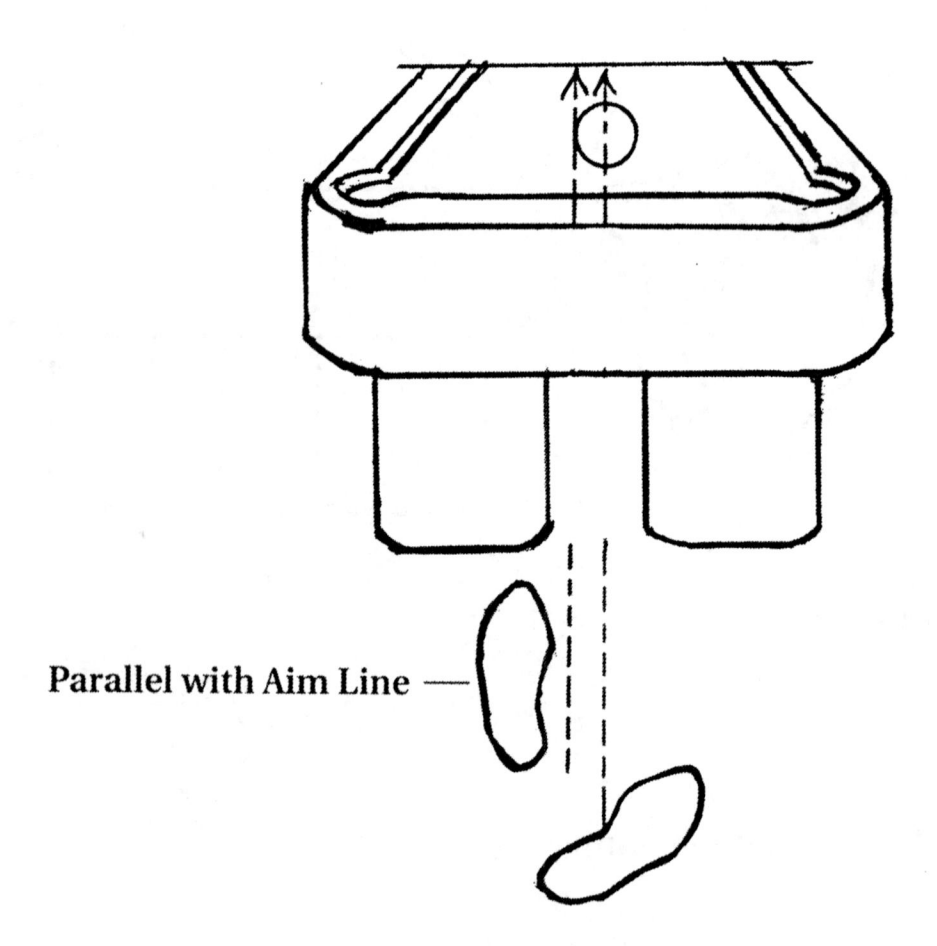

Parallel with Aim Line

Front Foot

Note: I refer to the ***left edge of the cue ball*** as my left foot's reference point. I wind up having my **Front Foot** a couple of inches to the left of the Cue Ball's Left Edge as it points *parallel* with the aim line.

***The final arrangement of the shooter's Feet is the result of the initial position combined with personal preference**.

Refer to my examples to help get you started, but then invest some time with **your own initial foot placements** with the floor's extended aim line. Use your own footings to suit your own needs. Because of everyone's different shapes and sizes, my personal alignment points will not be suitable for all.

You should continue monitoring your footing and their pivoting until you develop your subconscious "feel". You will need little awareness; once you find what comfortably works for you.

Don't be surprised if you find that you have an initial tendency to drift around with your footing and face/cue alignments. It will only be temporary, because your body will be learning to relax over the shot and, as a result, you will be slightly adjusting to find a comfortable alignment.

When searching for your body's **Focal Points** over the aim line, use the easiest way that you can to identify and remember them. Maybe you will find that your front leg works better as your initial footing. If you wish, see where your shoulder, chest and waist are located in relation to your initial footing.

I have a suggestion, if you don't play regularly, remember to align yourself straight with the proper initial footing and then try aligning your **Middle Alignment Guide Point** (top left tooth) over the aim line. Your body should remember the "feel" that you originally programmed and will adjust to the needed alignment position as you bend down. Perhaps you will feel the placement of the cue around your mouth area better than around your chin, or vice a versa.

Breaking down your individual areas of alignment is a needed investment on your part. When searching for your body's **Focal Points** over the aim line, use the easiest way that you can to identify and remember them. Maybe you will find that your front leg works better. Using *familiar body points* as your *alignment reference points* can only help you to help yourself when your pool, billiard, snooker, or bumper pool game goes awry.

Only a periodic checking of your alignment will be necessary, once you find **your** personal **Guide Points**. So, spend a little time in conscientious practice till you develop comfortable consistency to suit your style. Your comfortable alignment will become instinctive and you won't have to think about it when you are playing.

So, what is the significance of the body's **Focal Guide Points?**

Because, as you begin to develop a "feel" for proper alignment and aiming, you should 'see' that you will be *instinctively* relying, at least somewhat, on your favorite **Focal Guide Points** as a reference. I guess you can say that the **Facial and Foot Guide Points** are "instinctively important".

REMEMBER: The purpose of this chapter is to orient you with some important alignment elements and knowledge. In the overall scheme of shooting correctly and consistently, alignment is only one piece of the shooting package. Good aiming and stroking skills are needed, as well.

Outward - Inward Eyesight Angles

Do you still have problems with your aiming? Do you wonder why you cannot consistently shoot the cue ball in a straight direction? You know, the way you should be able to shoot.

Let me warn you that even if you align your body and head PERFECTLY over the shot every time ... It is still not enough!

Why is this statement true? Because with even a perfectly straight body and head alignment, your eyes can move around, unnoticeably, in their sockets. *Thus, your line of sight must be properly aligned, as well!*

Well, if you are having some difficulty, don't worry too much about it. I am going to share some of the overlooked "things" regarding the aiming of the cue ball, which should help.

First, there's an obvious question. How many objects do you say that you must aim when you try to sink an object ball? One? Two? Think about this a moment.

Almost everyone says two objects. The cue ball and the object ball. What do you say? Would you believe five objects? Okay, let's see.

The object ball is the target. That is *one* object.

The cue ball that hits the target is *two* objects.

Now, how about the cue stick? Don't you have to aim it correctly in order to send the cue ball on the proper path to the target? That's *three objects.*

Now, ask yourself; what aims the cue stick to the cue ball? The answer is you -- the shooter. How about your body? Don't you have to consider the direction (alignment) of your body, which holds and strokes the cue stick to the cue ball to the target? So, that would make it **four** objects that you must be aware of when you are shooting.

Five Objects to Aim

But, *because your eyes can move around independently within their sockets, it should help you to think that you have FIVE objects to consider when aiming!* This way you won't forget about addressing their line of sight. I think of my two eyes as one, because when our two eyes look at an object, our brain interprets the 3-dimensional picture as though we are using one eye. Our two separate eyes function as one.

When you look at only one object, you don't have to be concerned with the alignment of your body, head or eyes. But, in shooting a shot in the games of pool, billiards, or snooker it is different. Instead of aiming and aligning just one object, you have more. Most of the amateurs and a high percentage of the advanced players thought that there are only two objects on the table to aim. They said the cue ball and the target (object ball or a rail point). But as you've learned from my Alignment chapter, the cue stick is another object to aim.

So, in the game of pool, billiards and snooker, we must concern ourselves with three objects on the table and two off the table (body and eyes). The precise aiming of five objects is a much harder undertaking than simply looking at only one object. With one object, it doesn't matter if we have our **Nose Centerline**, or any other **Facial Point** aligned to the center of the single object, or to the sides of the single object, or wherever. We don't have to give this the slightest thought.

In pool there is a huge difference, because we must be concerned with the slightest turn of our face and eyes over the cue stick, in order to align properly over the aim line. The next thing we must be concerned with is where we are aiming the cue stick in regards to the cue ball and the aim line. And then we must be concerned with aiming the cue ball's required contact point to hit the target at its required point. So, as you can see, **our perception of our body and eye's alignment in relation to the aim line, cue stick, cue ball and the aim target is crucial.**

The process of aiming in pool, billiards, or snooker is not as easy as any pool freshman might initially think. *Most normal pool players have two separate eyes located on opposite sides of their Nose.*

OUTWARD-LOOKING-IN ANGLES

So, what does this obvious observation have to do with aiming in pool? The answer is *WE ARE LOOKING AT THE THREE SEPARATE OBJECTS ON THE POOL TABLE FROM TWO OUTWARD-LOOKING-IN ANGLES FROM FIVE POSSIBLE SIGHT LINES OF AIM*.

Think about that before you read on.

Line of Sight

Okay! The *__first__* line of sight can be with Two Evenly Focused Eyes with the **Nose Center Alignment** over the aim line. Remember that it will probably take a little time for you to learn how to focus your both eyes on the object, especially when you are not used to looking with Two Evenly Focused Eyes!

The *__second__* line of sight can come from the right eye with it directly over the aim line. I refer to this as the **"Pure Right Eye Aim"** using the **Rifle Shooting Alignment** over the aim line.

The *__third__* line of sight can come from the left eye with the left eye directly over the aim line. I refer to this as the **"Pure Left Eye Aim"** using the **Rifle Shooting Alignment** over the aim line.

The *__fourth__* aim line can come from a **Right Dominant Eye** with various alignment points across the face. (*Remember: A **Dominant Eye** is not the same thing as a **Pure Eye**. With the **Dominant Eye,** you are using two eyes, but one eye is more focused on the object than the other).

The *__fifth__* aim line can come from a **Left Dominant Eye** with various alignment points across the face.

These seemingly unimportant facts became precious keys that unlocked the doors, which changed my perspective on aiming forever. These simple "right-in-front-of-your-face" facts taught me that **there is much more to aiming than meets the eye!**

I eventually found that the separate outward/in eye angles, the five possible lines of sighting, the aiming of three objects on the pool table, the shooter's body on the floor, the eye's proper line of sight and the instinctive body turning made **STRAIGHT SHOOTING** an *hallucination* to me. It was a wonder that I ever made a straight shot!

See the following illustrations.

Illustration 22

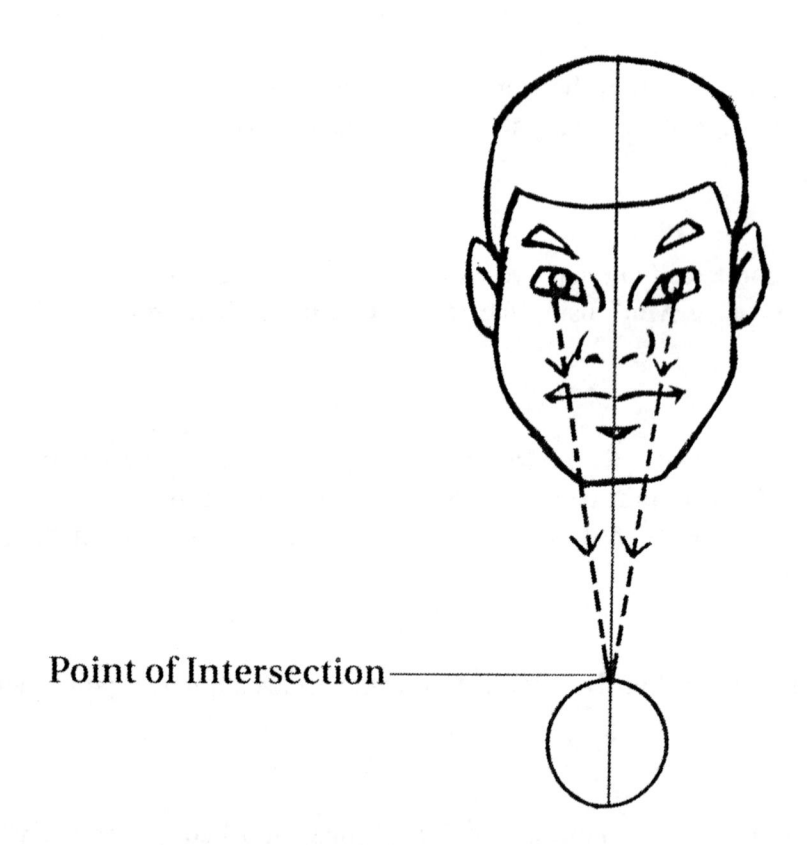

Intersection

NOTE: The head is straight and the nose is centered with the **Object's Center Point**. Each of the two eyes' straight lines of sight is looking *inward*! That means that the two individual straight lines of sight are originating from a point outside the **Nose's Center Point**. **Thus, the eyes are looking from an outward to an inward direction.**

Note Well: In Illustration 22 the two eyes are not starting their aim directly over the straight aim line from the **Nose's Centerline Point**, but their straight lines of aim both *intersect* on the aim line at the **Object's Center Point**.

Illustration 23

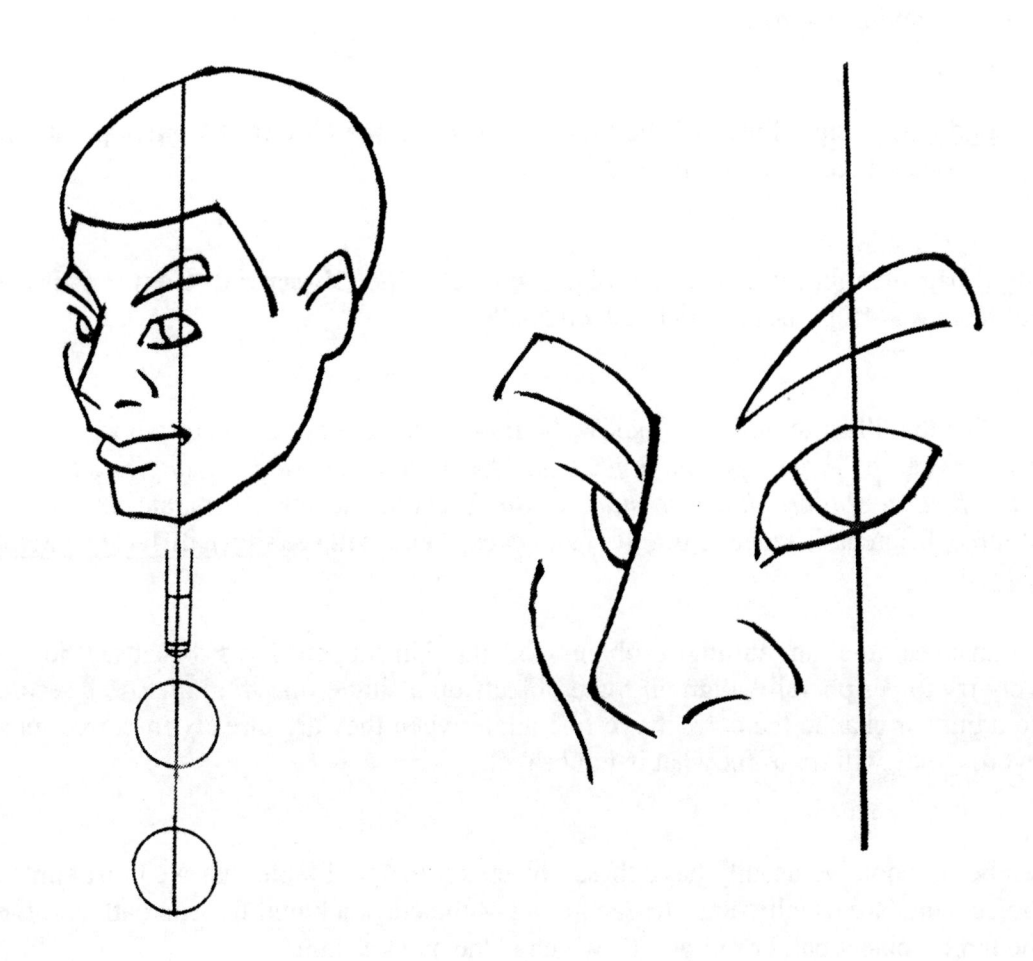

Note: The shooter's eye is directly over the cue stick. ***There is an advantage here because there is no outward/in sight angle to the Cue Stick Center Point, the Cue Ball Center point, or the Object Center Point***. The **Eye's Straight Sight Line** begins and ends on the *same* straight aim line through all three **Object Center Points**.

The above illustration is the **Rifle Shooting Alignment**. Even though this is an awkward and uncomfortable one for some of us, this cue/face alignment will provide a straight aim line starting from the single eye (for either eye), and then continue straight through all three **Object Center Points**.

Three Different Facial Guidepoints

Now, I want you to see in the following illustration that there are *three* separate pairs of straight sight lines originating from the eyes when individually focusing on three objects.

The first pair of sight lines will be looking *inward* at the cue stick center point, which is about 1/2 inch from the cue ball.

The second pair of sight lines will be looking *inward* at the **Cue Ball Center** point which is about (my personal) 2 feet from my face and eyes.

The third pair of sight lines will be looking *inward* at the **Object ball Center Point**, which are several feet away from the cue stick and cue ball.

Take notice that illustration 24 will show the nose is centered over the aim line; the eyes are looking (inward) at the *three separate objects and form three separate eye angles and will each intersect the face at slightly different places*. **So,** because the three separate objects will be located at three different distances from the face (eyes) - **you will see three different Facial Top Guide Points!**

This translates into an aiming problem for the Un-trained Eyes because they would instinctively try to peripherally align all three objects on a single line of aim! As a result, they will try to adjust or change the correct eye line angle when they are already in correct position. In other words, they will try to fix what is not broke!

Remember in pool, we usually have three objects on the pool table that we must aim. There are two objects that are usually close to each other -- the cue stick and the cue ball, and then the third is the target (object ball or rail point), which is the most distant.

Take a close look at the next illustration, which compares the eye sight angles when the off-centered eyes are looking at three object balls on a straight line, *but at different distances from the face*.

Illustration 24

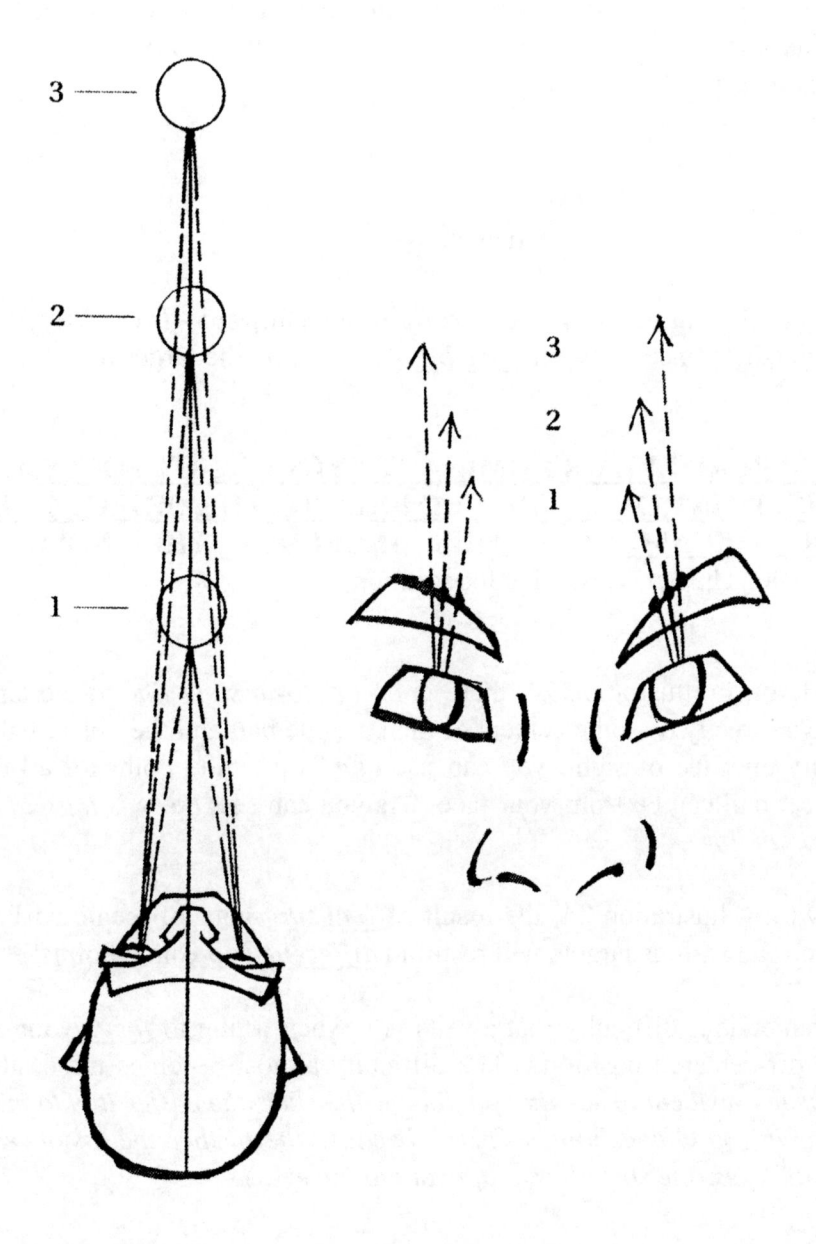

Note: The head is straight and the **Nose Centerline** is in line with the aim line through the center of the three objects. Compare the different eyesight angles with the **Straight Head**.

Note Well: The Facial Top Guide Points of the cue, cue ball and three object balls do not line up! Thus, three different Facial Guide Points!

Can you notice that in the Nose Centerline alignment, even, if you move the object ball on a straight line away from the cue ball and your face, the changing distance from your stationary face would cause the angle of your two eye's straight sight line to change? Yes, it should be true that by placing the cue stick at the same facial point for each shot, we will get the same eye angle to the cue ball and cue stick, because you usually set your body at the same distance from the cue ball. But, if you think about it, *the eye angle to the object ball will not always be the same, because of its different locations from the cue ball.*

Focusing

So, what precisely do I want you to *see* and learn in this Outward - Inward Eyesight Angles chapter? Recognize the difference between ***focusing*** your aim on the target from a centered and off-center position.

Remember: **YOUR PURE EYE OR DOMINANT EYE CAN NOT FOCUS THE SAME TOP FACIAL GUIDE POINT OVER THE CUE BALL TO THE OBJECT BALL FROM AN OFF-CENTER ALIGNMENT. THIS INCLUDES THE NOSE CENTER ALIGNMENT!** (See this chapter's last page for solution).

As I have showed you in illustration 23, there is no *out-to-in sight line* to the targets when aiming with a Pure Eye directly over the centers of the cue, cue ball and the object ball. And as a result of having only one line of sight, you can use **one** Top Guide Point for all the various distances that the object ball can be from your face. As you can see, *there is a great advantage in learning this style of aiming.*

However, as shown in illustration 24, the result of ***focusing*** your off-centered Pure Eye or Dominant Eye's aim on the various targets will result in ***different*** Top Guide Points!

Do you see the tremendous difficulty that awaits you when trying to ***focus*** your aim on the longer shots from an off-centered position? The difficulty almost becomes impossibility. (*To the untrained eyes it is less evident to see that the longer the shot; the easier it is to misjudge the correct line of sight and Top Guide Point. This is because the further the distance of an off-angled target is from the eyes; the straighter it appears to the eyes*).

Did you notice that up until now I have been saying that the difficulty in shooting straight occurs when you try to ***FOCUS*** your aim from an off-centered aim? (***By focusing, I mean the concentration of all your "visual attention" on an object point***).

Do you want to laugh?

For some unknown reason(s), I once thought that I would get one straight sight line starting from my face at the **Nose Centerline**, while aiming with my two outward-looking-in sight lines. (Take a look below).

Illustration 25

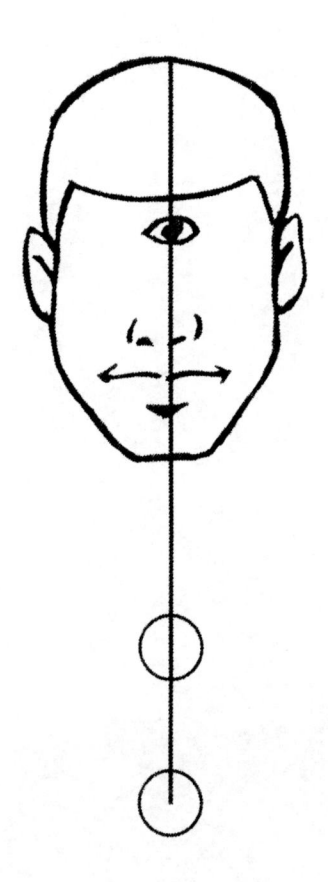

Fictitious Eye

Note: As you can see, this is a fictitious eye sight line! The **Nose Centerline** is directly over the straight aim line; there are no outside/looking in eye angles. The *Fictitious Eye* resides directly over the **Nose Centerline.**

I hope those of you who did laugh didn't laugh too hard, because this is a very good representation of what actually happens when you aim with the two balanced eyes in a Nose Center Alignment. Your two balanced lines of sight will see as "one centered eye".

*So, here lies the remedy for aiming with your two eyes in a Nose Centered alignment to more than one object, while enlisting the aid from your peripheral vision. Instead of *individually aiming* with your two out-to-in lines of sight and getting three separate Facial Guide Points; **Use Two Evenly Focused Eyes to intersect on the aim points and use only one Facial Guide Point – your Nose Centerline!**

Aiming The Cue Ball

This chapter's purpose is to alert those who are having problems with **shooting the simple straight shot** of some typical mistakes that they may be *naturally* committing.

As I mentioned in the Preface, "in order to shoot straight .... you must see straight". However, the "straight" I am referring to means seeing ***truly***, knowing what it really takes to perform our desired task and not what we blindly accept or guess.

Remember that I said that most amateur and advanced players would seldom align themselves over the shot the way that they intend? Well, the first thing that you will truly learn is that you cannot consistently make a straight shot without, first, making the cue ball go straight, consistently.

The Aim Starting Point

Well, now, I'm going to address one of the problems that support my statement by introducing **"The Aim Starting Point"**.

The Aim Starting Point refers to the precise location of your eyes in relation to the cue ball and/or aim line at the very beginning of your aim process. In other words, the place from where you actually begin to fixate your eyes. For example, it could be when you are directly over the cue ball center and aim line, or when you are not directly over them which will mean you will need to move some to adjust your aim. (Let me tell you; "almost directly over" is still not "directly over").

Because of all the various positions your two eyeballs can be in over the aim line, you need to have them in the same *seeing angle* when you begin your aiming process to get consistent results. Every time you finish one shot, your eyes will automatically change their positions to accommodate your viewing of the next objects. And after looking at different objects, located at changing distances from your face, as you walk around the table for your next shot, your eyes will not be in the exact angle needed for the beginning of your next aiming procedure.

The best way for me to show what I mean will be to compare the sight lines *initial* and *final* **Facial Top Guide Points**. By aligning your desired facial points over the same cue stick point, first, before, or at the same time that you start to focus on the cue ball, and/or aim line, ***you will be calibrating the angle of the eyes between the face and the target.*** **(See the following illustrations).**

Illustration 26

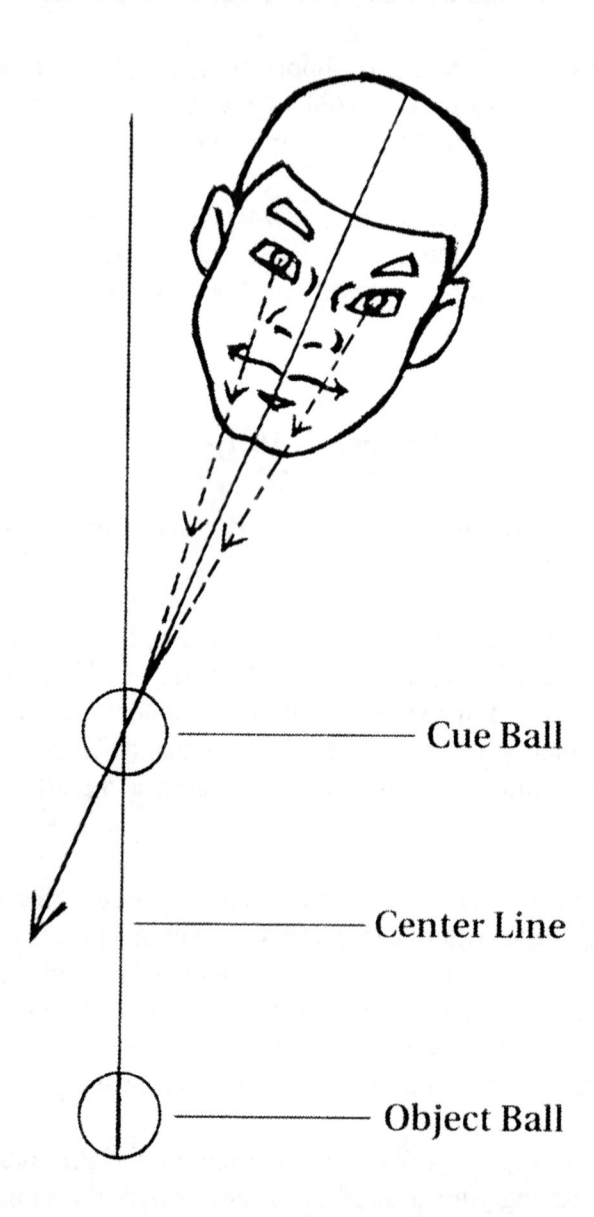

Note: In the above example, the shooter sees, with his Two Evenly Spaced Eyes, that his Nose Centerline is his *initial* Top Facial Guide Point from this position. His **Aim Starting Point** is located to the left of the cue ball center and aim line.

But watch what happens, as he moves to center his head over the shot while <u>continuing to fixate his eyes on the cue ball center</u>!

Illustration 27

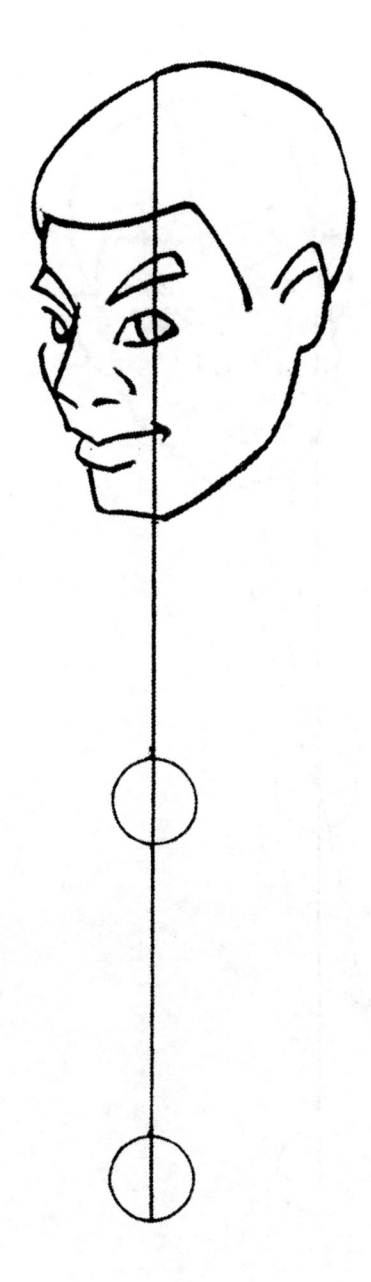

Top Guide Point

Note: In his final position, the shooter now sees that "**close to his Left Pure Eye's Brow Center**" is his *final* Top Facial Guide Point from this position.

His **Top Guide Point** has changed and his two eyes are no longer evenly spaced in relation to his Nose Centerline, **But here is where the trouble lies:** *Instead of, now, basing their aim along the sight line that intersects the NEW TOP GUIDE POINT, the untrained eyes will still aim according to their original Nose Center Alignment!*

Illustration 28

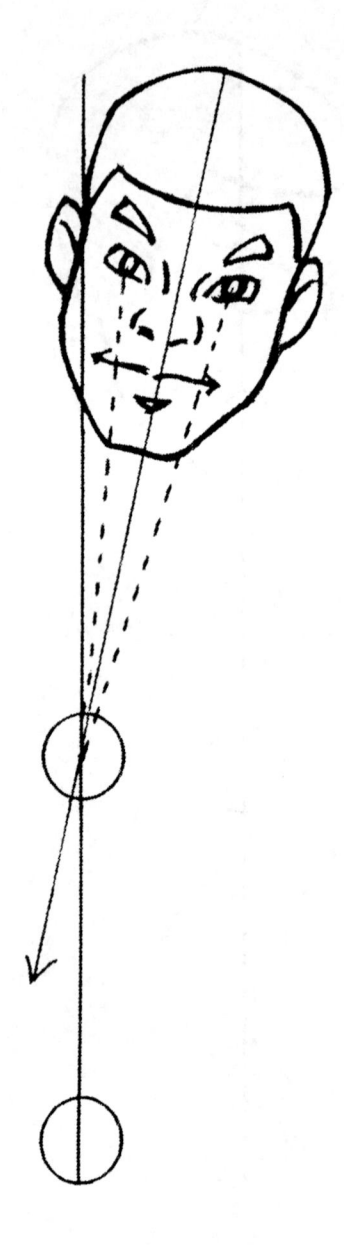

Note: In the above example, the shooter sees, with his Two Evenly Spaced Eyes, that his Nose Centerline is his *initial* Top Facial Guide Point from this position. His **Aim Starting Point** is still located to the left of the cue ball center and aim line, but it is closer to the cue ball center than the previous example.

Now, watch what happens this time, as he moves to center his head over the shot while <u>continuing to fixate his eyes on the cue ball center</u>!

Illustration 29

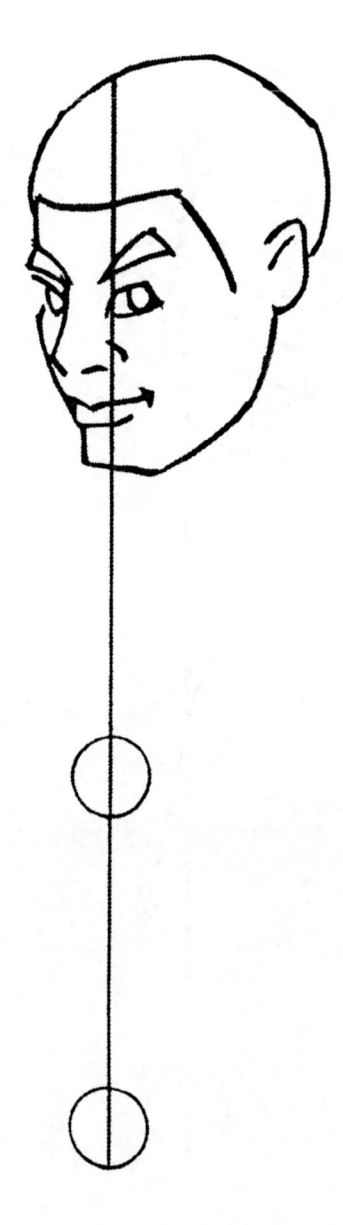

Note: In his final position, the shooter now sees that **"Left Eye Point"** is his *final* **Top Facial Guide Point** from this position.

His **Top Guide Point** has changed and his two eyes are no longer evenly spaced in relation to his Nose Centerline, **But here is where the trouble lies**: *Instead of, now, basing their aim along the sight line that intersects the NEW TOP GUIDE POINT, the untrained eyes will still aim according to their original Nose Center Alignment!*

Illustration 30

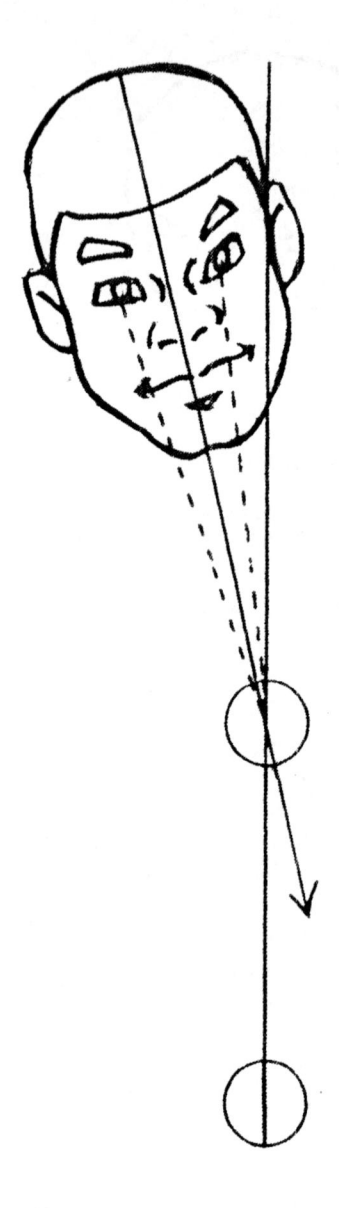

Note: In the above example, the shooter sees, with his Two Evenly Spaced Eyes, that his Nose Centerline is his *initial* Top Facial Guide Point from this position. His **Aim Starting Point** is now located **to the right of the cue ball center and aim line.**

Now, watch what happens this time, as he moves to center his head over the shot while <u>continuing to fixate his eyes on the cue ball center</u>!

Illustration 31

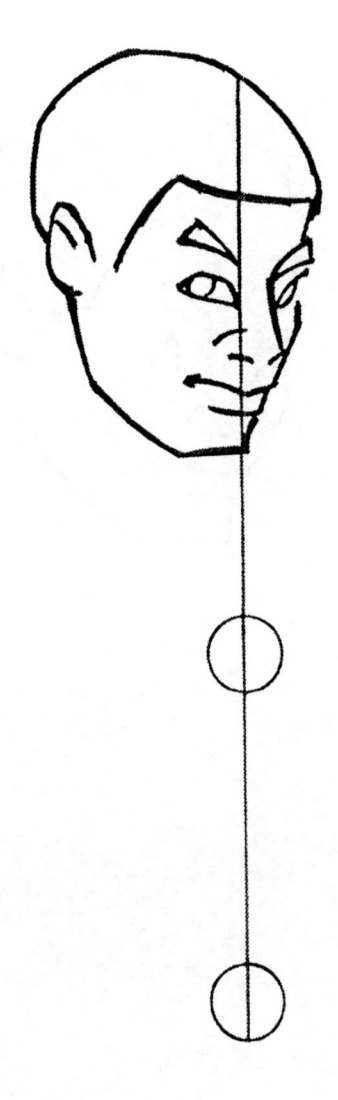

Note: In his final position, the shooter now sees that his **Right Eye Point** is his *final* **Top Facial Guide Point** from this position.

Again, his **Top Guide Point** has changed and his two eyes are no longer evenly spaced in relation to his Nose Centerline. **But here is where the trouble lies:** *Instead of, now, basing their aim along the sight line that intersects the NEW TOP GUIDE POINT, the untrained eyes will still aim according to their original Nose Center Alignment!*

Illustration 32

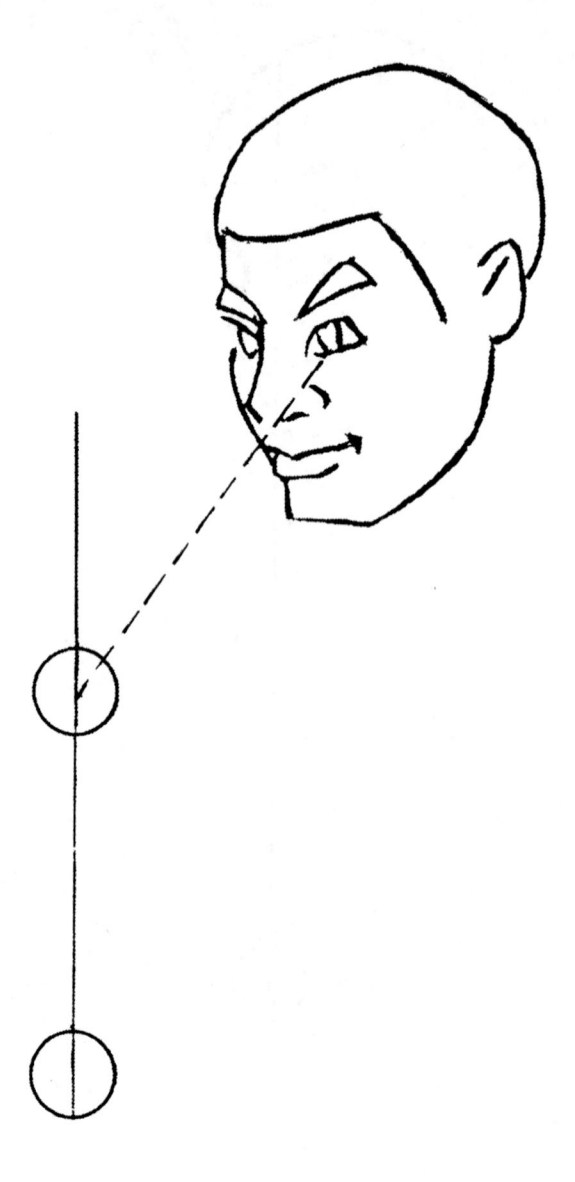

Note: In the above example, the shooter starts to fixate his **Left Pure Eye** on the center of the cue ball from an *unusually* wide position from the aim line. This is the result of the player beginning to focus while still walking towards the shot. Don't be in such a hurry! From this **Aim Starting Point**, he sees that his *initial* **Top Facial Guide Point** is the **Center of his Left Eyebrow**, which is directly above his centered eye.

Watch what happens to the angle of his eye with his face, as he moves to center his **Left Eye's Aim Perception**, while continuing to fixate on the cue ball center.

Illustration 33

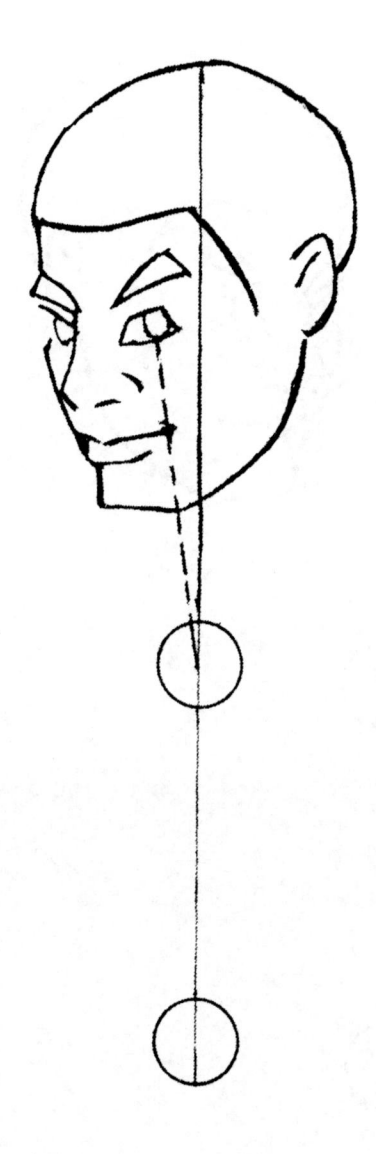

Note: In his final shooting position, the shooter sees that his *__final__* **Top Guide Point** has moved to the **far Left Edge of his Eyebrow**. Look at the wide angle his **Left Pure Eye** makes with his face now!

His **Top Guide Point** has changed and, although he realizes that his left eye's perception is *abnormal*, his trouble will unexpectedly surface when he tries to re-adjust his aim from this awkward position and alignment! *The shooter would be far better off to just get up and start over from the center of the aim line.

Illustration 34

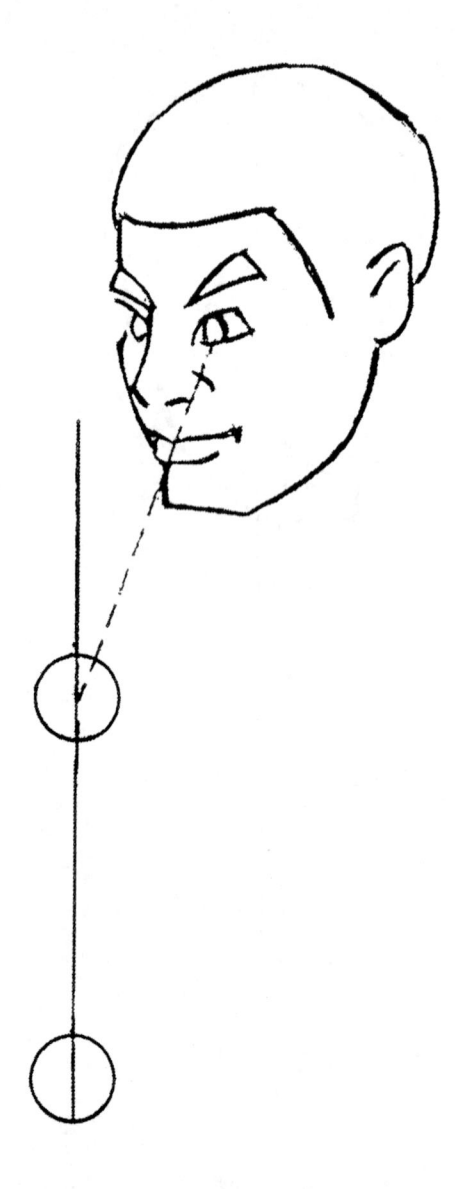

Note: Here the shooter's **Aim Starting Point** is closer to the aim line than the previous illustration and he is still using his **Left Pure Eye** to start his aiming. But look at how his left eye is angled inwards toward his nose. His **Top Facial Guide Point** is to the **Right of his Left Eyebrow Center**.

Now, watch what happens with this very skilled or very lucky shooter, as he continues to fixate his eyes on the cue ball center!

Illustration 35

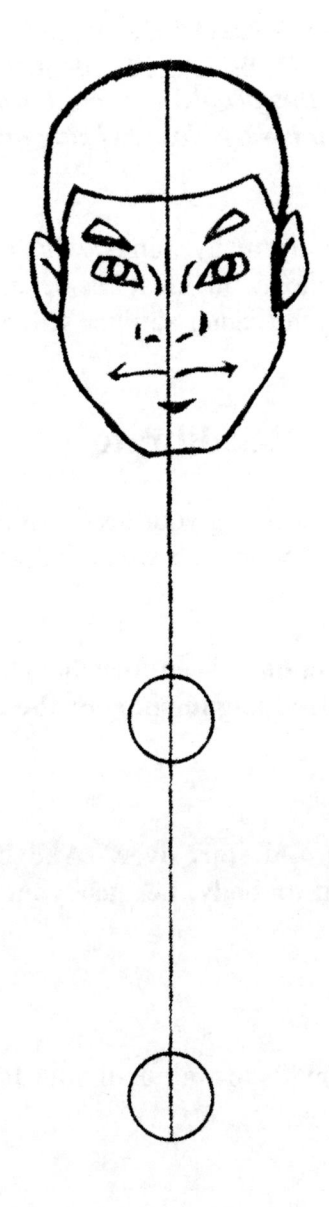

Eye Switching

Note: In his *final* shooting position, he is, now, properly centered over the aim line for his **Two Evenly Focused Eyes** in his **Nose Center Alignment**! During his final adjustment for his shooting position, the shooter knowingly, or unknowingly employed the subtle and overlooked – *****Eye Switch**.

*Whether he intended to switch his eyes, or not; Eye Switching is definitely not a reliable practice. *Do not start aiming with one eye and end up with a different one!

Please be alerted to the fact that the principle of the changing Top Guide Point applies to all the alignments!

Mostly, I wanted you to see that the hidden trouble lies in keeping your eyes fixated on the cue ball and/or aim line, while you move your head to center your aim from an off-centered position! *Understandably, this problem is very hard for the untrained eyes to detect when the shooter's Aim Starting Point is very close to being actually centered.*

You should understand that there are many things, which can individually, or collectively contribute to distorting our aim perception. But, as far as bending down straight over the shot is concerned, the slightest deviation from the center aim line will affect your judgment.

Recalibrate

If you do find that you are turning or tilting your head, while you are bending down or when you are fixating your eyes on your aim point, you would be better off to *re-calibrate* your eyes by:

Looking away from the object you have been focusing on for at least a split-second, and then adjusting your face to your desired alignment over the cue stick and aim line.

OR

Do what I think is best: **Get up and start over. And be careful to go straight down without turning or tilting your head or body, because your eyes start their fixating while you are standing up!**

So, the best way to "Start your Aim" is to wait until your favorite alignment is directly over the aim line before you start to focus.

And remember not to switch your eyes during your aim process, because you will be changing your line of sight from your face to the object.

Dominant Eye

I think, that the **majority of shooters who are having difficulty shooting straight are unknowingly using a Dominant Eye**! And they just don't realize that they are seeing with an out-to-in angle of sight instead of with a centered line of sight.

A **Dominant Eye** sees more on its outward/inward line of sight than the other eye. A **Dominant Eye** is not the same thing as using only one (pure) eye. By using only one eye (from the eye itself starting over the whole imaginary line through the **Cue Ball Centerline** to the target), I mean that the other eye is not involved in the process of aiming. But a **Dominant Eye** (starting its aim from a point outside the imaginary aim line) could be seeing from 51% to 99% of the target, while the other eye is involved in the process of aiming.

I believe that nearly every human being normally uses a **Dominant Eye** or a **Pure Eye** to look at things in their daily lives. We *naturally* resort to seeing things with the 'least effort' regarding our eyes, because trying to see with two evenly spaced eyes takes some deliberating, especially when you want to train them to consistently aim one spherical object to another for each shot.

For years, I erroneously thought that I understood **Dominant Eye Aiming**. My blind loyalties to my **Dominant Eye** and to my more comfortable alignment were unnecessary and potent ingredients in my failure. If only I could have found comfort using the **Pure Eye Aim**, or, even the **Two Evenly Spaced Eyes** with the **Nose Center Alignment**, I would not have shot like I was cursed! Yes, I know my "pool scars" are my own faults: **That's** *why I wrote this book after years of personal struggle and research – to help you avoid these common mistakes and bad habits.*

At this point, you should know that if you are aligned over the straight shot with your **Nose Centerline,** then your two separate eyes are looking from two separate outward to inward angles to the cue ball center. And the only way to aim the **Back Cue Ball Center Point** along the straight imaginary line to its target, in the **Nose Center Alignment**, is to use *Two Evenly Spaced Eyes*. That's because Two Evenly Spaced Eyes will intersect their two outward-looking-inward lines of sight on the **Object Ball's Center Point,** while *peripherally* aiming the cue and the cue ball at the same time. (For those who don't know, the following illustrations will show what is meant by peripheral vision).

Illustration 36

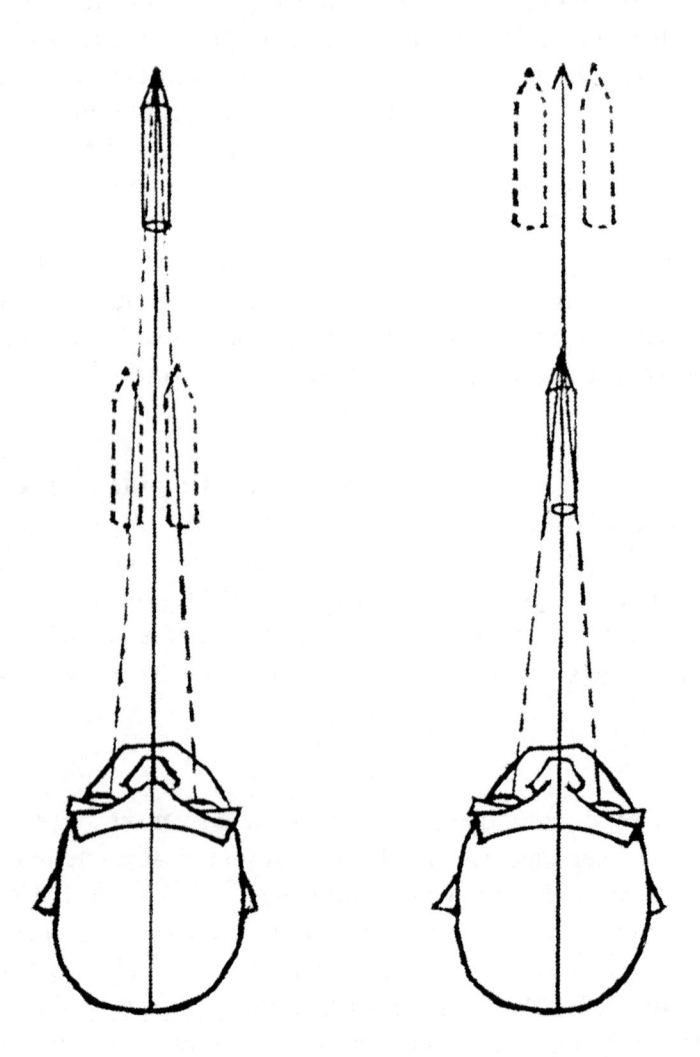

Peripheral Vision

Note: The illustration above has a total of two objects; one is on top and the other is at the bottom. A's side is showing that when the shooter fixates his balanced aim on the top object from a **Nose Center Alignment**, he is *peripherally* seeing two objects at the bottom.

B's side shows the shooter's *peripheral vision* sees two top objects while he focuses on the bottom object.

Illustration 37

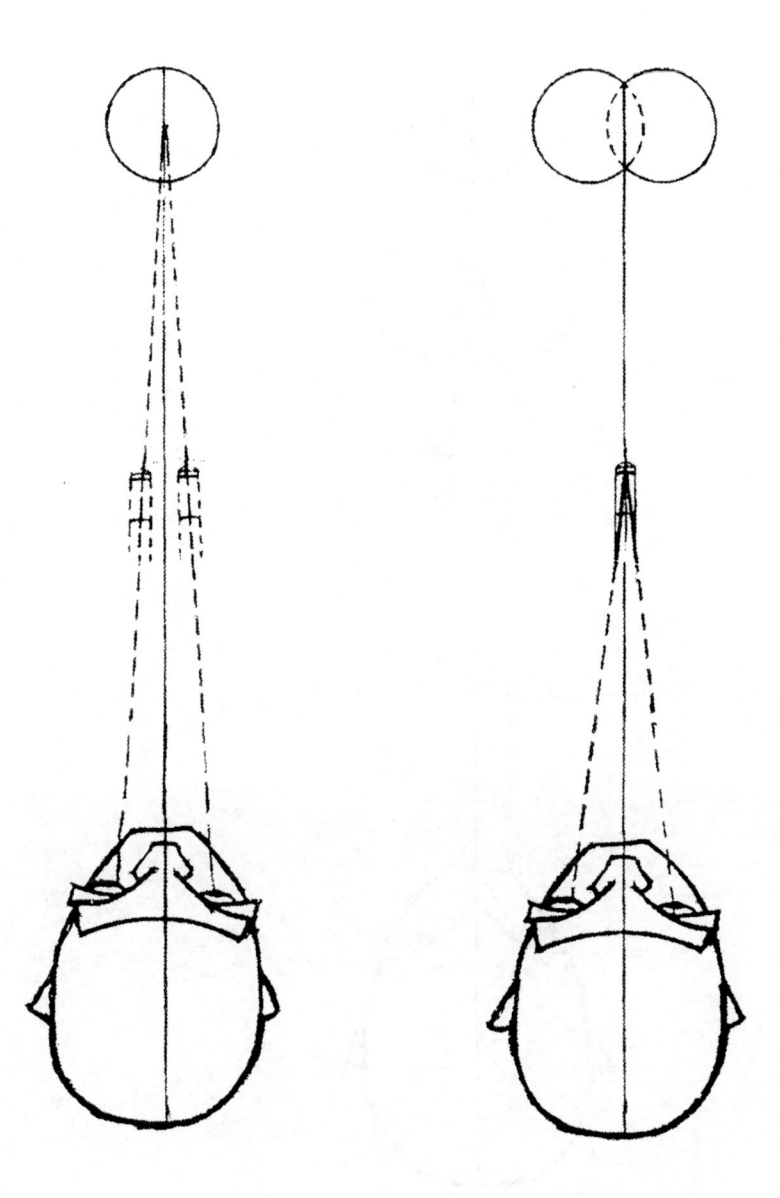

Note: Here I substituted the pencil shaped objects with the cue-tip and cue ball. The shooter, still in the **Nose Center Alignment**, will *peripherally* see two cue-tips when his **Two Evenly Spaced Eyes** focus on the cue ball in A.

In B, he *peripherally* sees two cue balls while fixating on the cue-tip with his **Two Evenly Spaced Eyes**.

Illustration 38

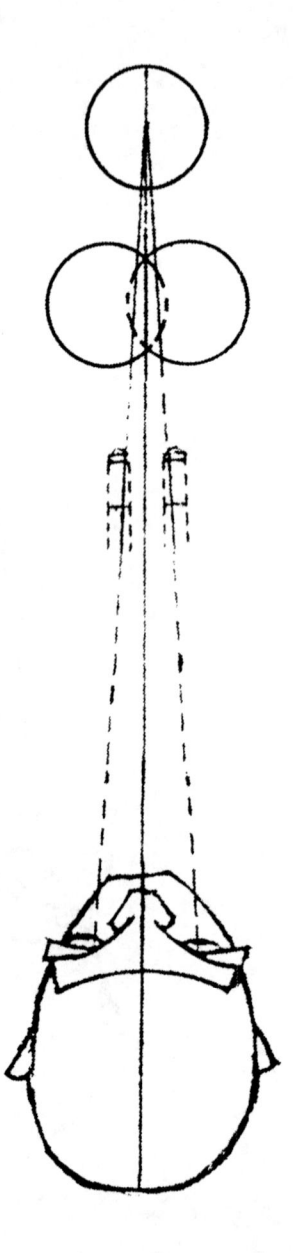

Note: In this final peripheral example, I've added another ball for a total of two balls and one cue-tip. However, when the shooter focuses his balanced aim on the top ball from a **Nose Center Alignment**, his **peripheral vision** will see two cue balls and two cue-tips below.

It is harder to *peripherally* see the two balls because of their spherical shape, but if you look for them, you will *peripherally* see them!

Aim Compensation

I found that, after years of trying, I just could <u>not</u> aim the **Back Center Point** of the cue ball (the side facing the shooter) to the target and be consistently successful.... Unless, I was using Two Evenly Spaced Eyes in the **Nose Center Alignment**, or used a **Pure Eye Aim** in the **Rifle Shooting Alignment**. Even though, I learned these Aims and Alignments, I still had difficulty, because I was always instinctively returning to <u>**my**</u> natural way of aiming, which is with a **Dominant Eye**. (A Dominant Eye's line of aim can lie anywhere between the Pure Eye and Two Even Eye lines).

You can not **focus** your aim through the same **Back Cue Ball Center Point** in a straight shot, <u>with a **Dominant Eye or a Pure Eye**</u>, the same successful way that you can <u>with the Two Evenly Spaced Eyes</u> using the ***same Nose Center Alignment***!

You need to aim compensate when you focus your aim using a **Dominant Eye** or a **Pure Eye** in the **Nose Center Alignment**. And the amount of aim compensation that you make depends precisely on the outward/inward sight angle to the aim line. The **Eye's** outward/inward angle depends on the distance your **Eye** is away from the aim line. This is because distance determines the size or width of an angle.

Let's refer back to the mirror demonstration. Do you remember you had to remain frozen in your alignment over the aim line and then squint both eyes, and then try using the two different **Dominant Eyes**?

Do you remember that for each separate way of using (seeing) your eyes, you were seeing the cue stick align with slightly different facial points? Well, the sight angles from your different eye positions will be different, **because your eyes' (Pure or Dominant) origin of sight are each located at *different* distances from the aim line.** <u>Thus, different distances need different aim compensations.</u>

Did I shock you by what I just said?

Balanced Aim

When shooting a **Straight Shot**, the **Cue Ball Center** and **Object Ball Center** are directly over the imaginary aim line. So, when using only one (Pure) eye to aim the **Cue Ball Center**, your one eye will be directly over the whole imaginary line - from the eye to the target. Now, with the Two Evenly Focused Eyes in the **Nose Center Alignment** over the aim line, the two outward-looking inward eyes will *intersect* its "**balanced aim**" on your target! (See Applications chapter for another aim method with two balanced eyes in the Nose Center alignment).

Note: Your two eyes are not starting their individual line of sight directly over the imaginary line from a **Nose Center Alignment**. So, remember when aiming to the **Cue Ball Center Point** with a **Pure Eye,** or a **Dominant Eye**, using the **Nose Center Alignment**, <u>*you need to make an aim compensation to your target.*</u>

Those two ways of aiming and aligning (Pure Eye and Two Even Eyes) through the **Cue Ball Center Point** would probably solve most of all the aiming problems, if everybody would shoot this way. And that is where, I believe, most of the aiming mistakes are hidden from the one-nighters, amateurs and some advanced players. **The majority of the aiming flaws are hidden from sight**.

There are probably tens of millions of players that, like me, ***CAN NOT GET COMFORTABLE IN THE NOSE CENTER OR THE ONE-EYE ALIGNMENT POSITIONS!*** Our natural aiming preference is with a **Dominant Eye**. Whether we use a <u>slightly</u> **Dominant Eye** or a <u>mostly</u> **Dominant Eye**, it is still dominant! *Another way of looking at is - the Dominant Eye Aim is the Two Eye Aim with their center (Nose Centerline) aligned off-center!*

So, if you were among the <u>successful shooters</u> from the Straight Shooting Test, who aligned their **Nose Centerline** over the cue ball and the imaginary aim line, and who **actually** <u>*focused* your **aim through the Cue ball Center**</u> to the center of your mark on the rail, you might not have realized it, but <u>you were aiming with Two Evenly Spaced Eyes.</u> Good! That means your hard training is paying off. (If that's what you were trying to do Use Two Even Eyes).

And if you were among the <u>successful shooters</u> that aligned their *Nose Centerline* over the cue ball and the imaginary aim line and <u>did not *focus* your aim</u> with Two Evenly Spaced Eyes, then give yourself a big one-handed clap for your pool ingenuity or lucky guessing, because you had to be aiming by either:

1   your Right or Left **Dominant Eye** to the cue ball with <u>some amount of aim compensation</u>. Meaning that you were **not** aiming the exact **Cue Ball Center Point** to the exact **Object Ball Center Point** because your Dominant Eye was aiming from out to inward.

2   your Right or Left **Pure Eye** to the cue ball with <u>some amount of aim compensation</u>. Meaning that you were **not** aiming the exact **Cue Ball Center Point** to the target, because your **Pure Eye** was aiming from out to inward.

And, if you were **not** in the **Nose Center Alignment** over the Cue Ball Center and aim line, (among the endless arrays of alignments and eye aiming combinations) you could have aimed directly to the target with:

3   your Right or Left **Dominant Eye** to the **Cue Ball Center Point** to the target <u>with aim compensation</u> while in various face/cue alignments. Meaning you were not aiming the exact Cue Ball Center to the exact Object Ball Center because your Eye was aiming from out to inward.

4   your Right or Left **Pure Eye** to the center of the cue ball to the Object Ball Center <u>with no aim compensation</u> while in the **Rifle Shooting Alignment** because your straight line of sight was directly over the aim line.

My point in showing you these examples are to caution that there are many different ways to get confused when you attempt to aim straight, even with trained eyes!

For me, trying to aim with Two Evenly Spaced Eyes seems 'unnatural' and uncomfortable. I would constantly tire my eyes from the striving to *evenly focus* them. And how often do you see people using one **Pure Eye** walking around squinting their one eye in everyday lives? We naturally use both eyes that God gave us, while either eye sporadically takes turns being pure or dominant: *Eye Switching*.

What does this all have to do with shooting a cue ball straight? Let me begin by showing the five basic face/cue stick aim/alignments with their line of sights.   (Review the following illustrations).

Illustration 39

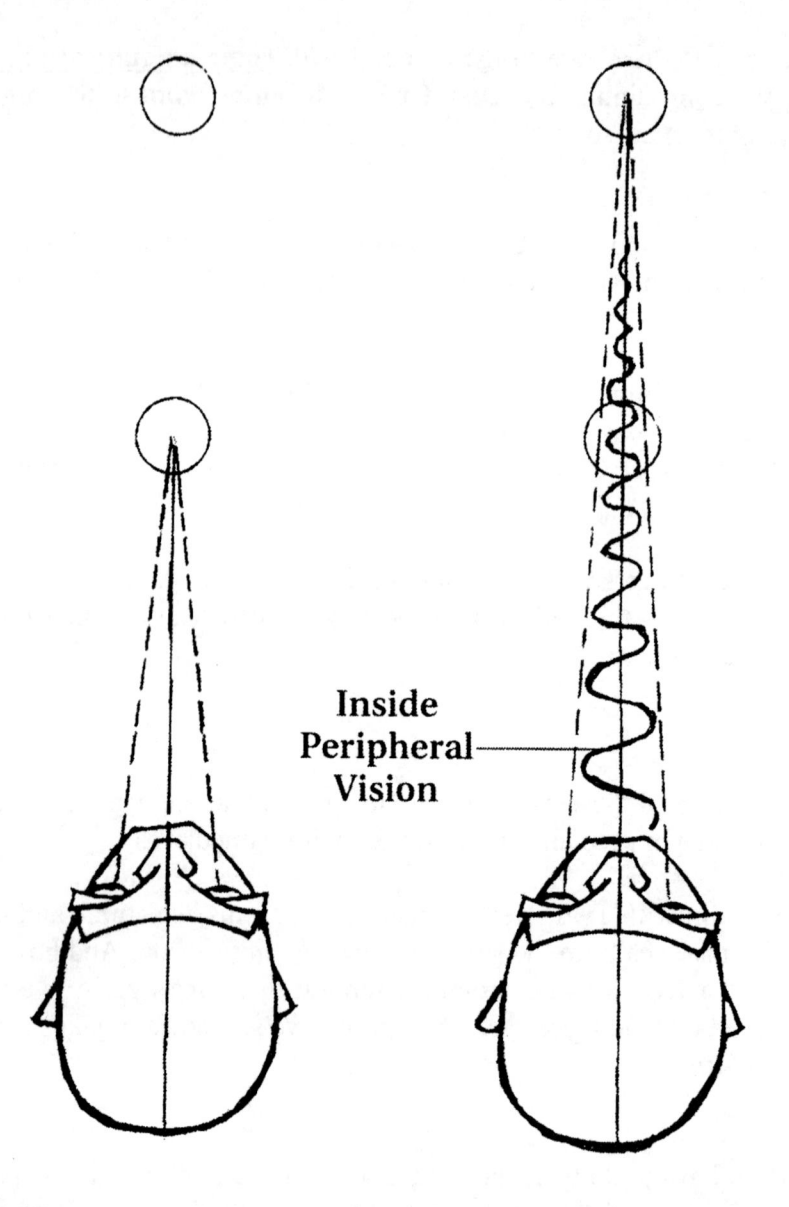

NOTE: Because the **Cue Ball Center Point** is directly over the imaginary aim line in this straight shot, the **Two Evenly Spaced Eyes** start their aim process by *intersecting* on the **Cue Ball Center in A.** As they switch their focus to the **Object Ball Center in B**, they will pass their *"balanced aim"* through the Cue Ball to the **Object Ball's Center Point, while their inside peripheral vision aims the cue and cue ball.**

As you can see, the **Jaw Center Point** is directly over the cue stick and the imaginary line. *No aim compensation is needed*.

Illustration 40

— Object Ball

— Cue Ball

— Right Pure Eye Aim

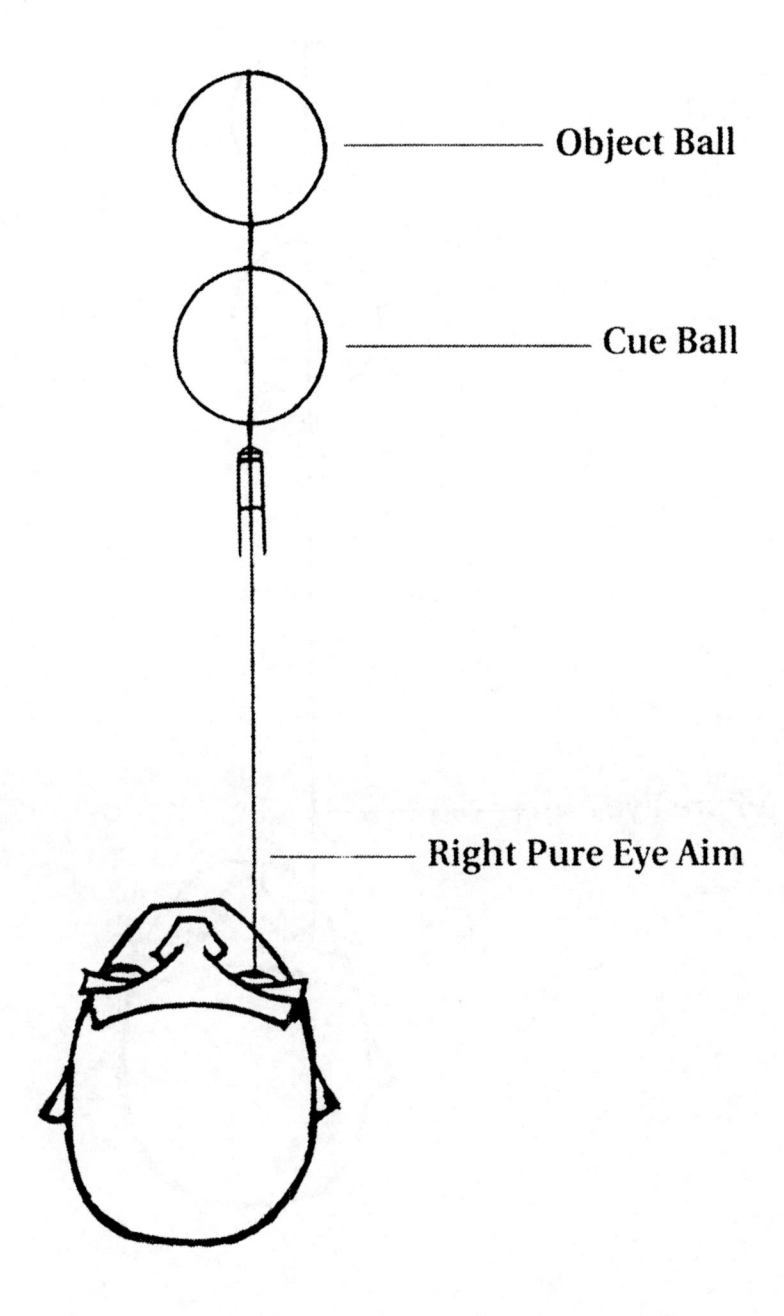

NOTE: The second example has the shooter's **Right Pure Eye** aligning directly over the cue stick and imaginary aim line. The Eye aims through the **Cue Ball Center** to the **Object Ball's Center Point**. The head is turned so that the right edge of the jaw is over the left edge of the cue stick. *<u>No aim compensation is needed</u>*.

Illustration 41

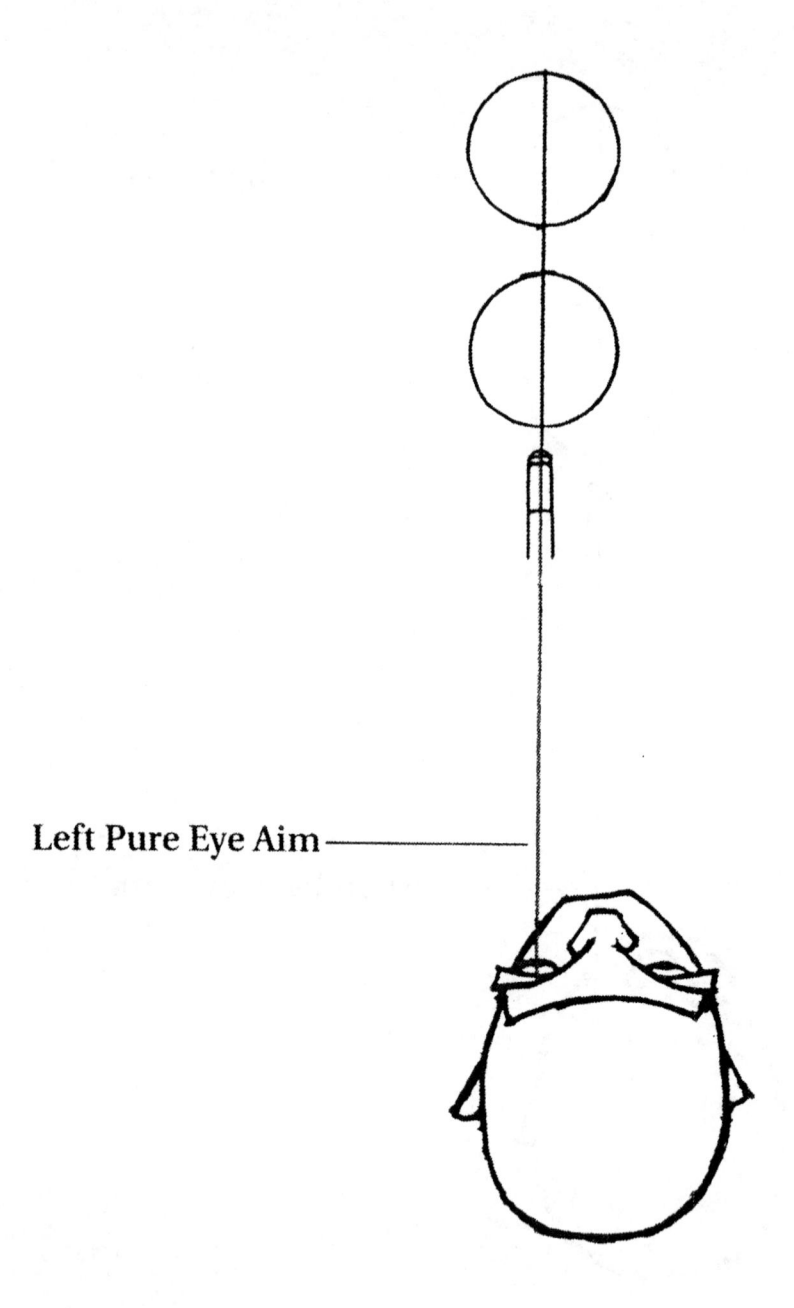

Left Pure Eye Aim ─────

   NOTE: The third example is showing that the **Pure Left Eye** is aligned directly over the cue stick and the imaginary aim line. The Eye aims through the **Cue Ball Center** to the **Object Ball's Center Point**. The head is turned, so that the left edge of the jaw is over the right edge of the cue stick. *<u>No aim compensation needed</u>*.

Illustration 42

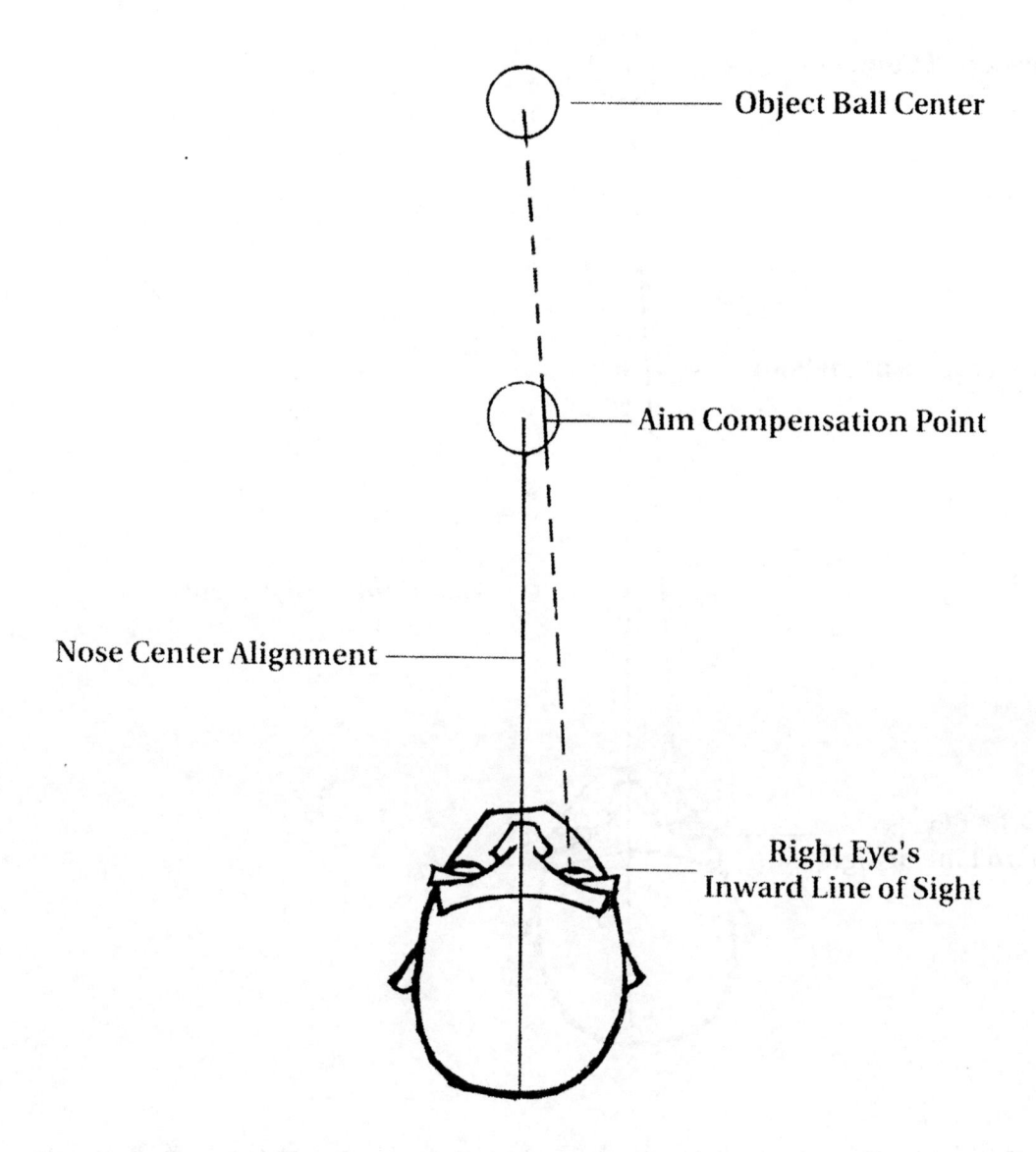

Note: This fourth example is showing that in the Nose Center Alignment the **Right Pure Eye** is *starting its outward/inward line of aim* from the right eye itself and continues straight through the cue ball. The **Pure Eye** *does not start its aim* over the **Cue Ball Center** or the imaginary aim line. Thus, the **Pure Eye** is aiming through a point on the cue ball that *meets the needs for an aim compensation* for this particular alignment.

Illustration 43

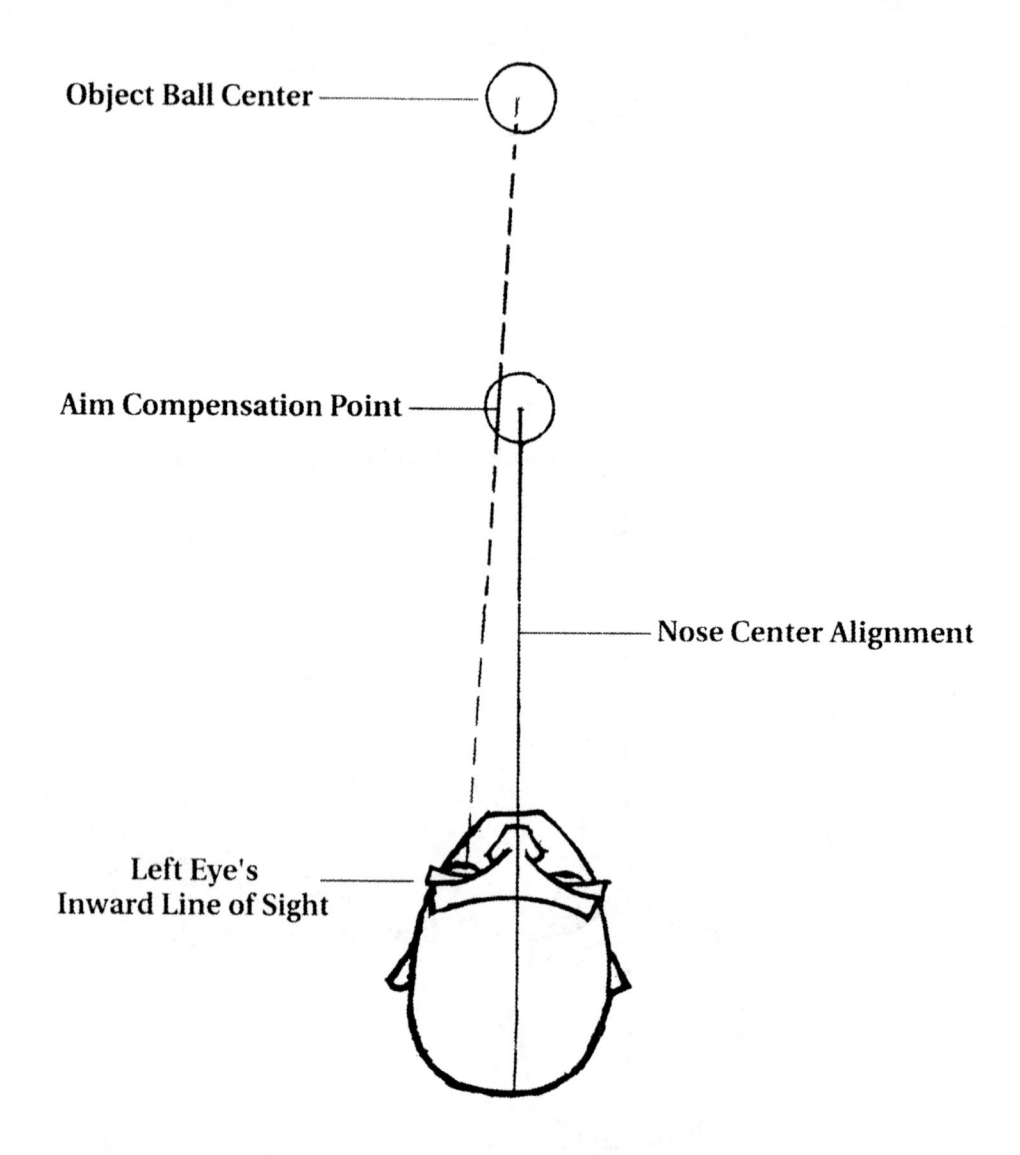

Object Ball Center ──────○

Aim Compensation Point ──── ○

Nose Center Alignment ──────

Left Eye's Inward Line of Sight ─────

NOTE: This fifth example shows that from the Nose Center Alignment the **Left Pure Eye** is *starting its outward/inward line of aim* from the left eye itself and continues straight through the cue ball.

The **Pure Eye** *does not* start its aim over the Cue Ball or imaginary aim line. Thus, the **Pure Eye** is aiming through a point on the cue ball that *__meets the needs for an aim compensation__* for this particular alignment.

74

Illustration 44

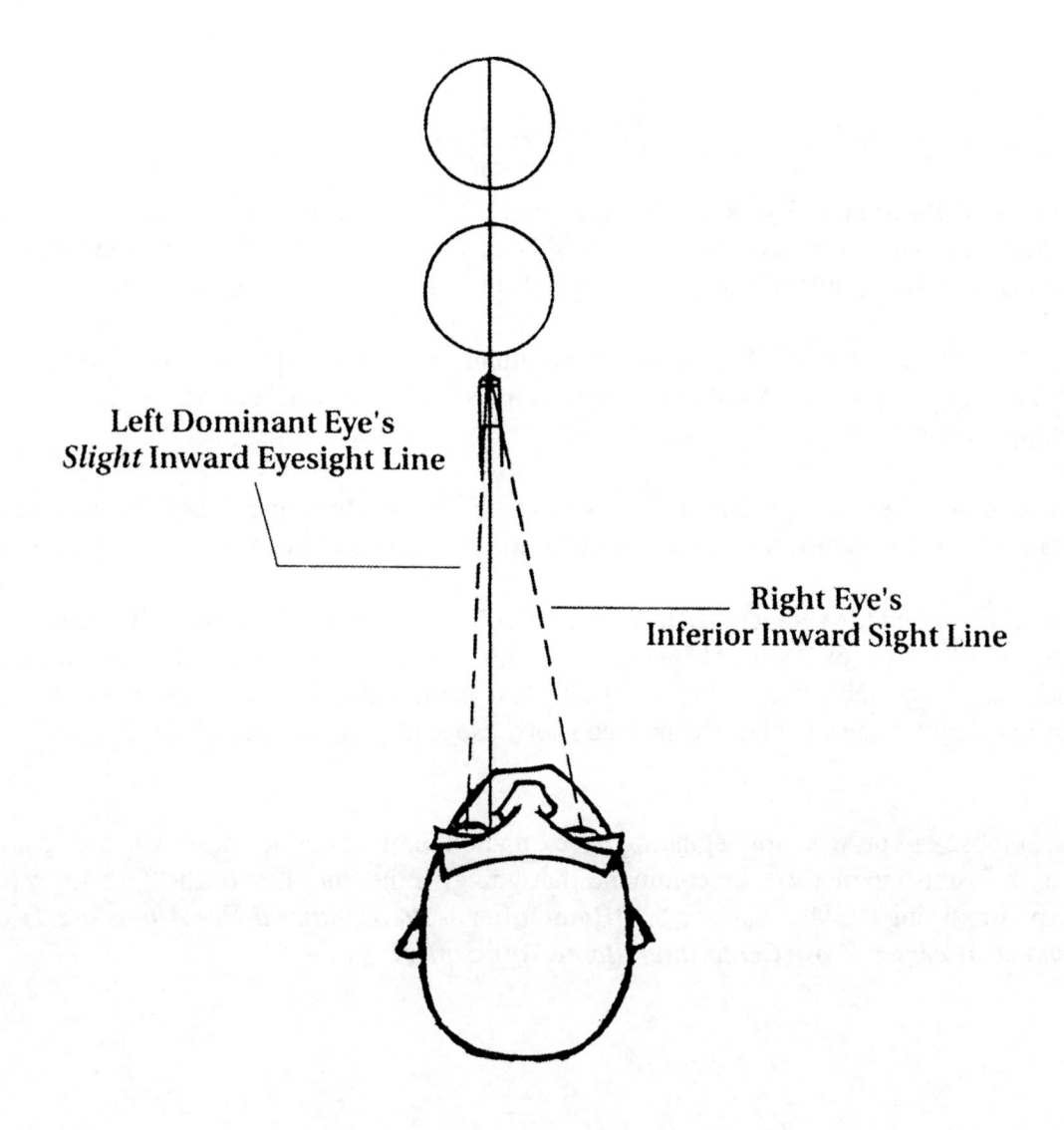

Dominant Eye Alignment

Note: In this final example, the shooter has **his Left Dominant Eye's Sight Line** and his **Right Eye's Inferior Sight Line properly synchronized** from this particular off-center alignment.

Even though the both eyes are synchronized in this example, I believe that the **Dominant Eye Alignment** is the hardest of the three aim alignments to learn for the UN–trained Eyes. This is because it is extremely difficult to differentiate between a 51% and a 57% dominance of an eye. Let me explain what I mean.

Let's say that for every shot there is a 100% focus total. For example: A Pure Eye will see 100% of the shot while the Two Evenly Focused Eyes will split their amount, so that the Right Eye will see 50% and the Left Eye sees 50%.

Inferior Eye

Now, the **Dominant Eye's** percentages have a wider scope than the two ways just mentioned. As I already stated, the range could be anywhere from 51% to 99% dominant which, also means, that the complementary percentage of the **Inferior Eye** is 49% to 1%.

Here's an example: If a Left Eye is 55% dominant then the complementary percentage must be - 100 minus 55 = 45%.   Another example is a 65% Dominant Eye needs a (100 – 65 = 35) 35% complement.

Can you see the extreme difficulty it would be to recognize the subtle fluctuations of a Dominant Eye and matching it's complement for the UN–trained Eye, as well as, for the experts?

How about when the shooter's Left or Right Eye's "usual 60% dominance" has inadvertently changed to 68%, or 69%, or 58% etc.?   And don't forget the needed complementary percentages. Remember, it only takes the slightest deviation from the required Dominant and Inferior Eye Sight Angles to cause a "missed shot", especially for the longer shots!

So, to those of you who are beginning to learn about aiming and to those who are looking to improve their existing method, I recommend that you give the Pure Eye or the Two Even Eyes a chance before trying the Dominant Eye. ***Remember: - the Dominant Eye Aim is the Two-Eye Aim with their center (Nose Centerline) aligned off-center!***

The Real Cue Ball Center

Of all the aim requirements the shooter faces regarding the task of shooting the cue ball straight, no other is more basic and important than precisely locating **The Real Cue Ball Center.** It is the very foundation for consistency in all pool, billiard, snooker and bumper pool games.

At first, it would be understandable to assume that only after a "little practice" this prerequisite could be easily mastered. After all, the balls are not moving around the table when you shoot. They are like cows grazing in the pasture - simply motionless.

However, when one considers that the shape of the balls are spherical and the calculating of the center points is usually attempted by the UN-trained Eyes from an off-centered alignment, it becomes more likely to conclude that they are facing a more formidable challenge than one's primary assumption.

Take the process of calculating the Cue Ball Center Point, for example, with the shooter aligning his Nose Centerline over the centered aim line. I'm sure that you would agree that is much easier to find the ball's center point by visually bisecting the left and right edges instead of only referring to one point.

If you do your calculating with a Pure Eye or a Dominant Eye from a Nose Center Alignment, you will be judging the edges of the ball from an out-to-inward eye position. What am I saying?

I'm saying that, if the shooter begins visually bisecting with their Left Pure Eye (for example) from a Nose Centered Alignment, they will really be seeing *more of the area behind the ball's left edge and less of the right edge than, if their Pure Eye was centered over the ball*. And what makes this subtlety hard to detect for the UN-trained Eye is the fact that they will still see a complete spherical object.

Apparent Center

I call this perception of this left eye's view – **The Apparent Cue Ball**. And here is where the basic mistake is made, if from a Nose Center Alignment you use your Left Pure Eye to visually bisect the Left Pure Eye's Apparent Edges, you will get – *A Left Apparent Center*. It's not the same **Real Center** you get when your Pure Eye is directly centered over the aim line. Of course, the same thinking applies to the Left Dominant Eye, Right Pure Eye and the Right Dominant Eye, which bisects from an out-to-inward line of sight, too. **YOU WILL GET AN APPARENT CENTER POINT!** (Take a look at the following Real and Apparent Center Examples).

Illustration 45

A
Rifle Shooting
Alignment

B
Nose Center
Alignment

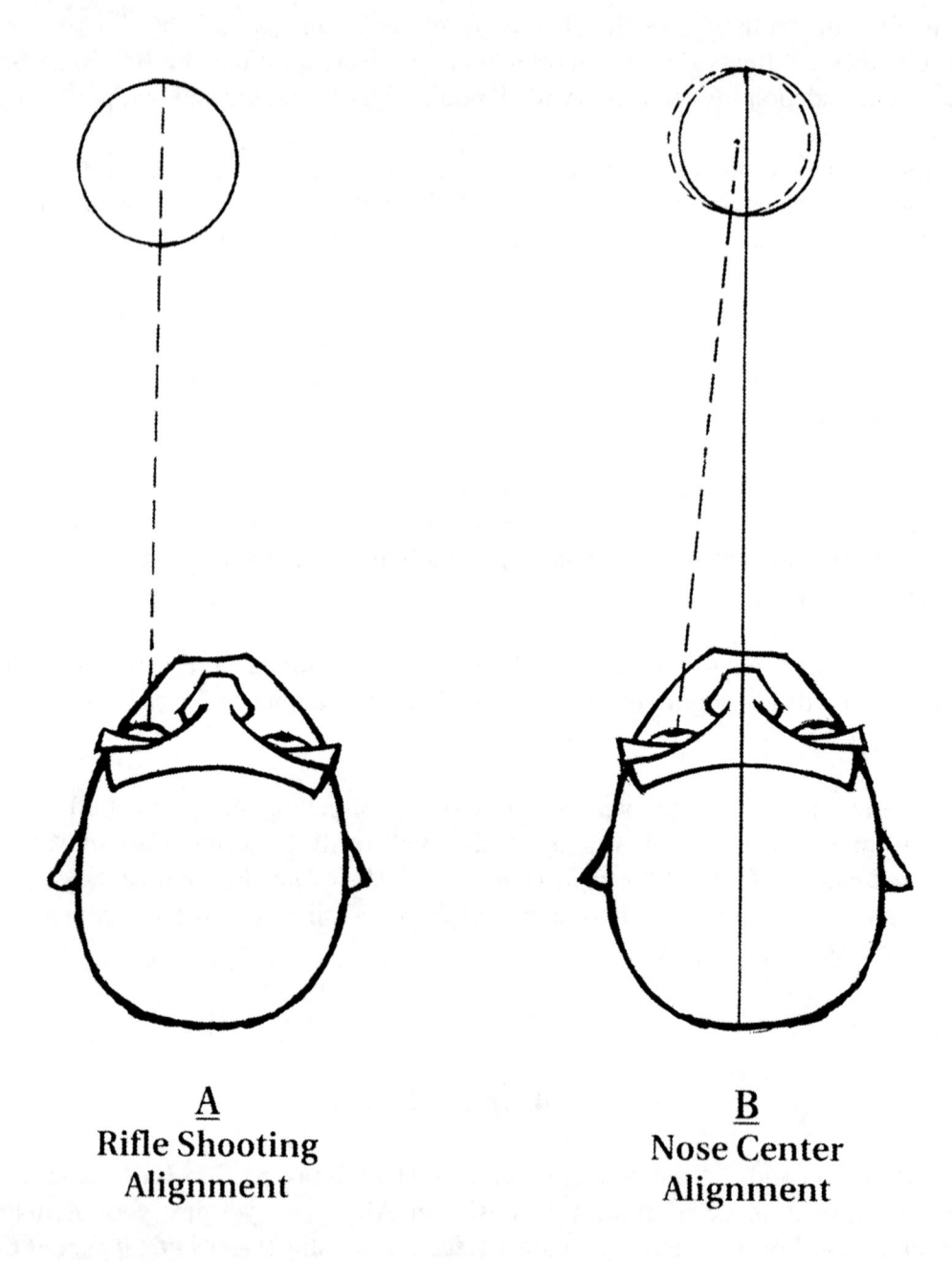

Note: Side A is showing the shooter aligned directly over the aim line and Cue Ball Center with **his Left Pure Eye**.

Side B is showing that the shooter is still using his **Left Pure Eye**, but from a **Nose Center Alignment**, his **Left Pure Eye** sees a **Left Apparent Cue Ball Center Point**!

Illustration 46

A
Rifle Shooting
Alignment

B
Nose Center
Alignment

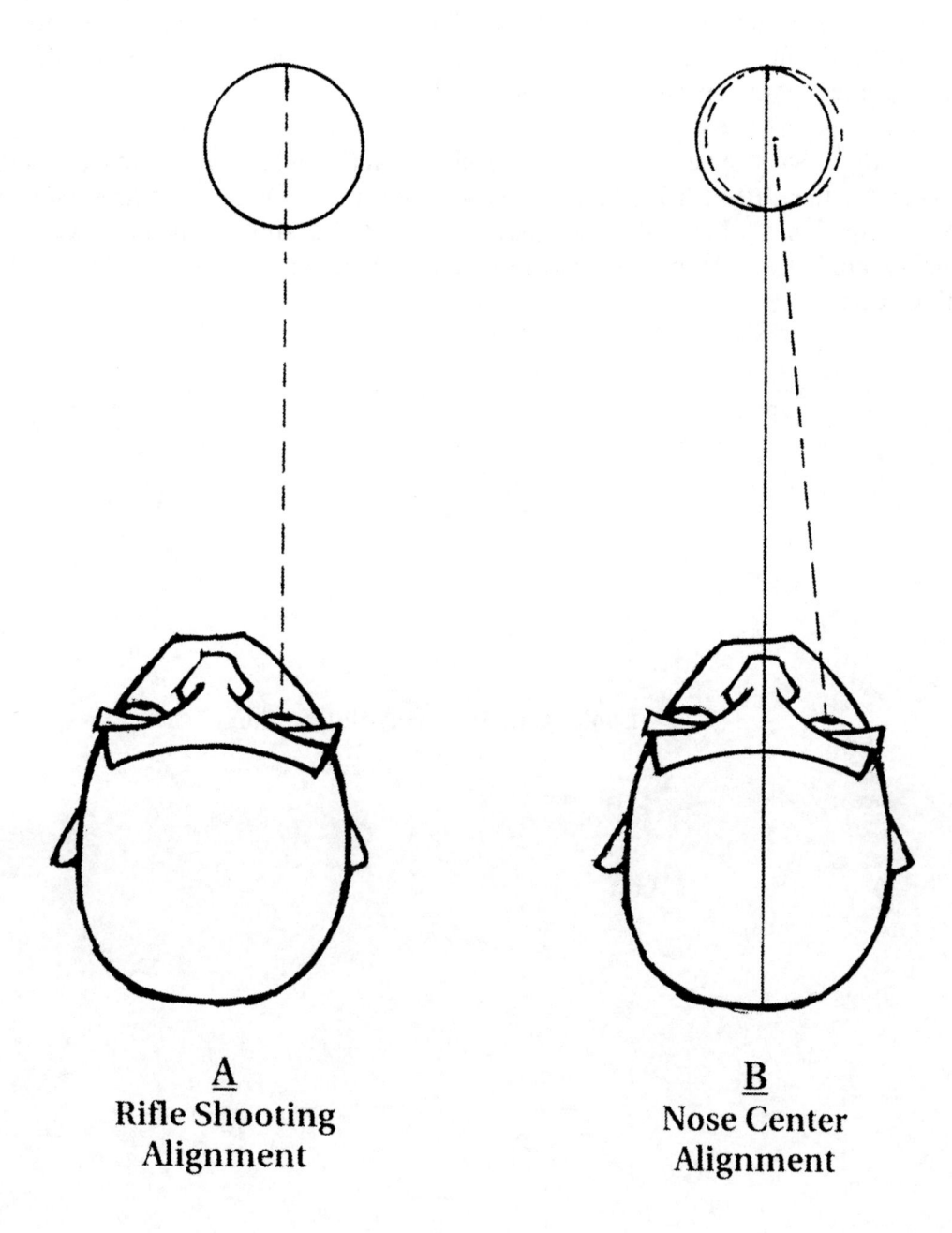

Note: Side A is showing the shooter aligned directly over the aim line and cue ball center with **his Right Pure Eye**.

Side B is showing that the shooter is still using his **Right Pure Eye**, but from a **Nose Center Alignment**. His **Right Pure Eye's** bisecting with the **Apparent Cue Ball** (dotted lines) yields a **Right Apparent Cue Ball Center Point**!

I've been stressing the importance of knowing the difference between aligning your aim from a centered position as opposed to an off-centered position for a good reason.

Do you now "see" that with the Pure Eye and Two Evenly Spaced Eyes aligned directly over the center ball and aim line, there are no aim compensations needed? But with the off-centered aims and alignments, you need aim compensations?

That's why I said, even if the successful shooters with The Straight Shooting Test compensated for their off-centered aiming, chances are that the majority didn't know precisely what they were doing. I say this, because those that did aim compensate were probably, unknowingly, aiming with their aim compensation based on what appeared to be **The Apparent Cue Ball Center**.

Look at the following illustration.

Illustration 47

Apparent Object Ball Center

Apparent Cue Ball Center

Nose Center Alignment

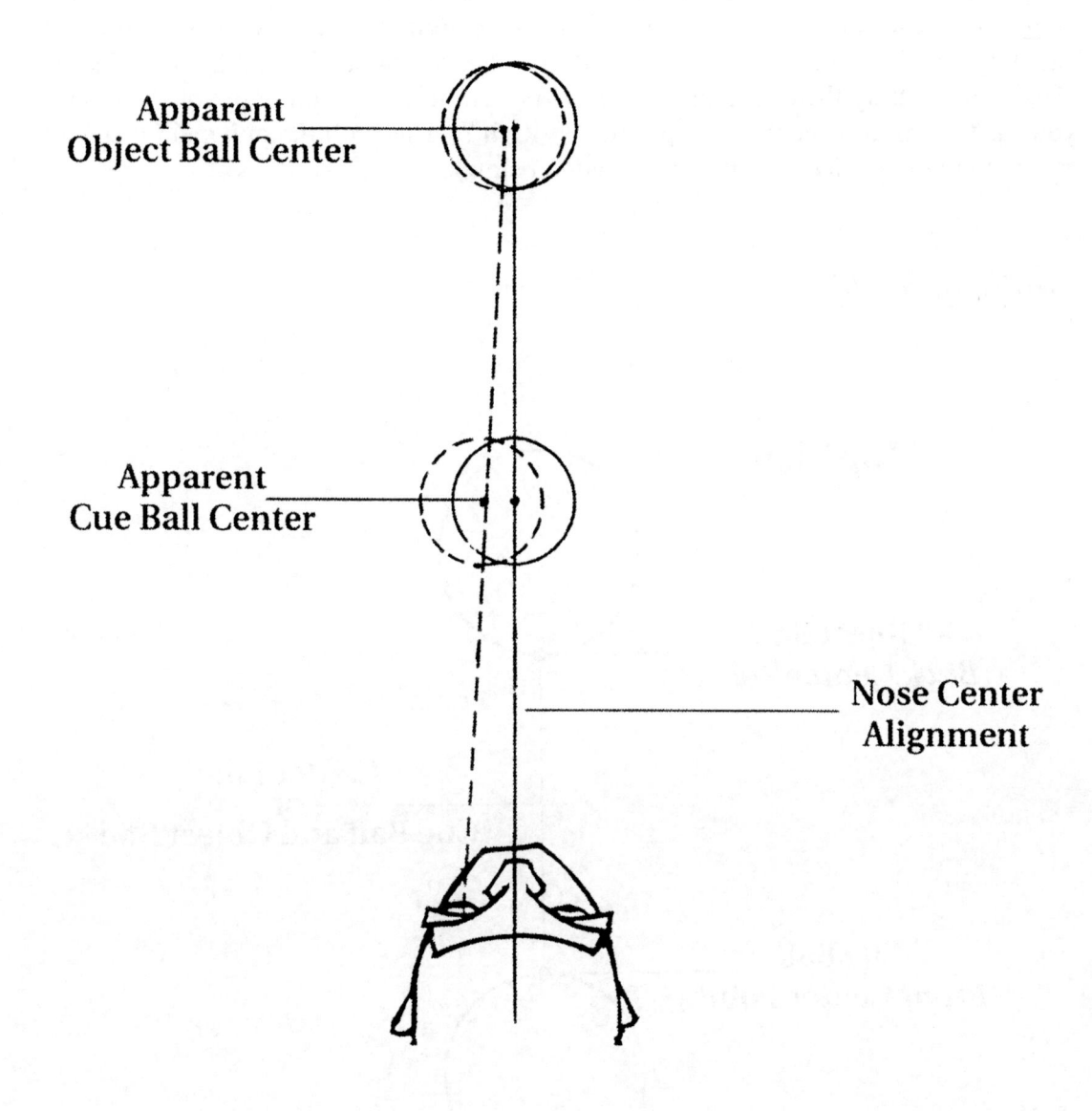

Note: The shooter is <u>making the mistake</u> of trying to shoot the **Left Apparent Cue Ball Center** to the **Apparent Object Ball Center** from an off-center alignment!

Another subtle aiming mistake is aiming the **Apparent Cue Ball Center** to the **Real Object Ball Center**!

I have a simple way that can help you to properly aim the Cue Ball Center. It begins with the explanation of the **Real Cue Ball Center Point**.

The **Real Cue Ball Center Point** that I will show you to **base** your aim on is <u>not in plain sight</u> when you are standing up behind the **Cue Ball**, or, even when you are down in your shooting position. You cannot see it while you are positioned behind the **Cue Ball** during your shot, but it is truly there. Sound strange? After all, how can you **base** your aim on a point that you can't see from your shooting position? Right? Have a little faith and I'll show you what I saw with my *Pool Eyes*. (See the illustration below).

Illustration 48

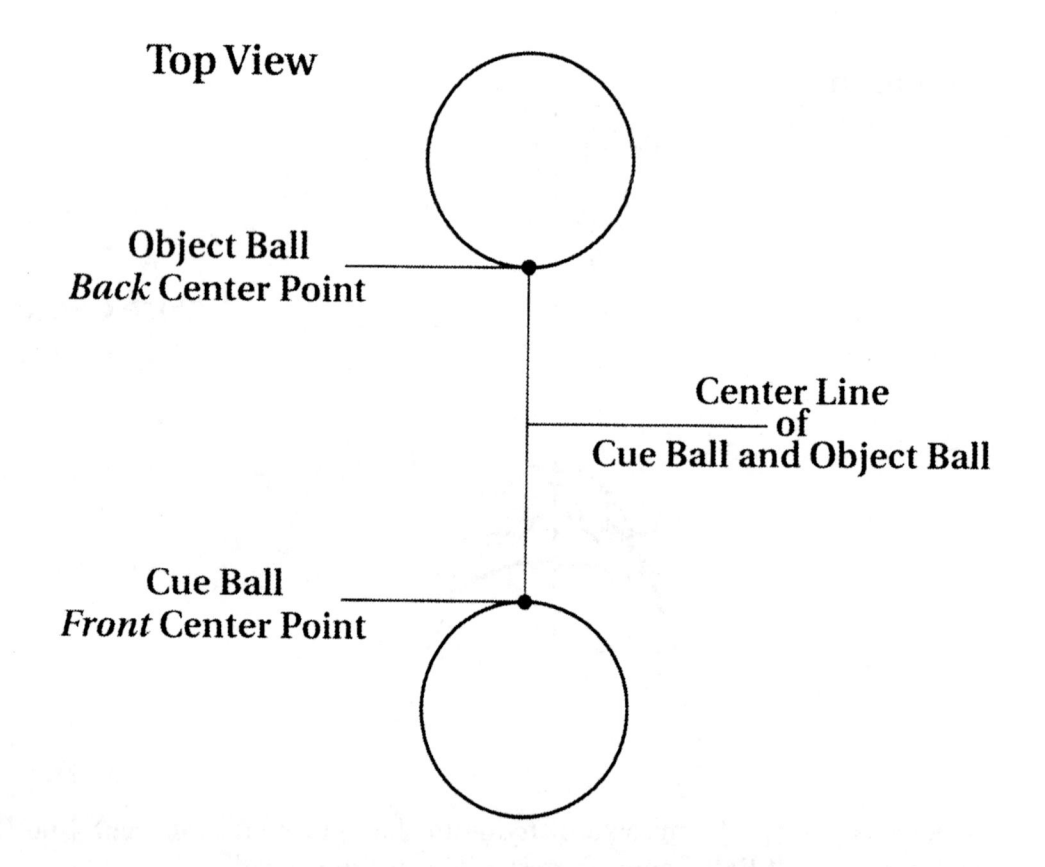

Top View

Object Ball
Back Center Point

Center Line
of
Cue Ball and Object Ball

Cue Ball
Front Center Point

Front Center Point

Note: In this straight shot illustration, the **Cue Ball Center Aim Points** that I am referring to is the <u>contact point</u> located on the **Real Equator**. The **Cue Ball's Contact Point** is located on its **Front Center Point**, which is out of the shooter's plain sight, while the **Object Ball's Contact Point** is facing the shooter on it's **Back** side.

The next point of importance when aiming the Cue Ball Center is the **Top Vertical Point**. (See Below).

Illustration 49

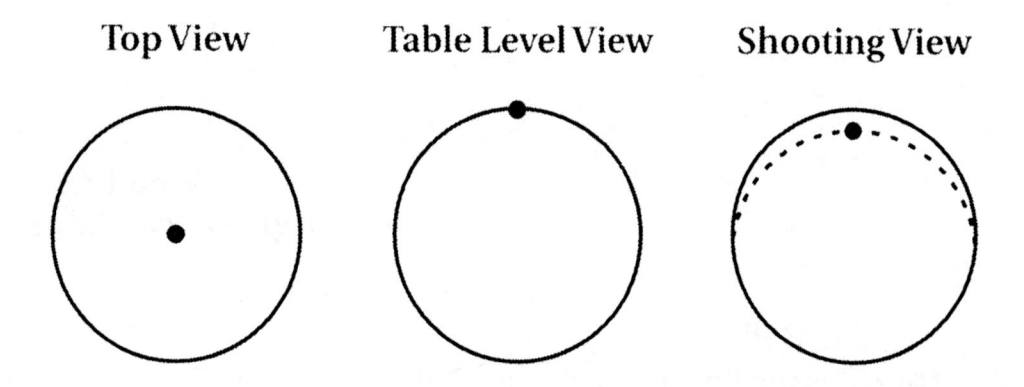

Top View   Table Level View   Shooting View

Top Vertical Point

Note: The appearance of the *height* of the **Cue Ball's Real Top Vertical Point** to the shooter on the **Cue Ball's Centerline** is the direct result from the eye's height above the **Cue Ball**. Compare the differences with the height on the **Cue Ball's Centerline** when viewed from the eye's standing angle and the eye's shooting position angle.

Note: The standing angle's **Real Top Vertical Point** *appears* to be located *lower* on the **Cue Ball's Centerline** than the shooting angle's aim point. This is why a person who stands 6'6" will see under *his* **Real Top Vertical Point** at a lower position on the **Cue Ball Centerline** than a person who is 4'6". The taller person will see more of the area behind the **Real Vertical Top Point**.

Illustration 50

Shooting View

Object Ball
Back Center Point

Cue Ball
Top Vertical Point

Cue Ball
Front Center Point

Cue Ball
Back Center Point

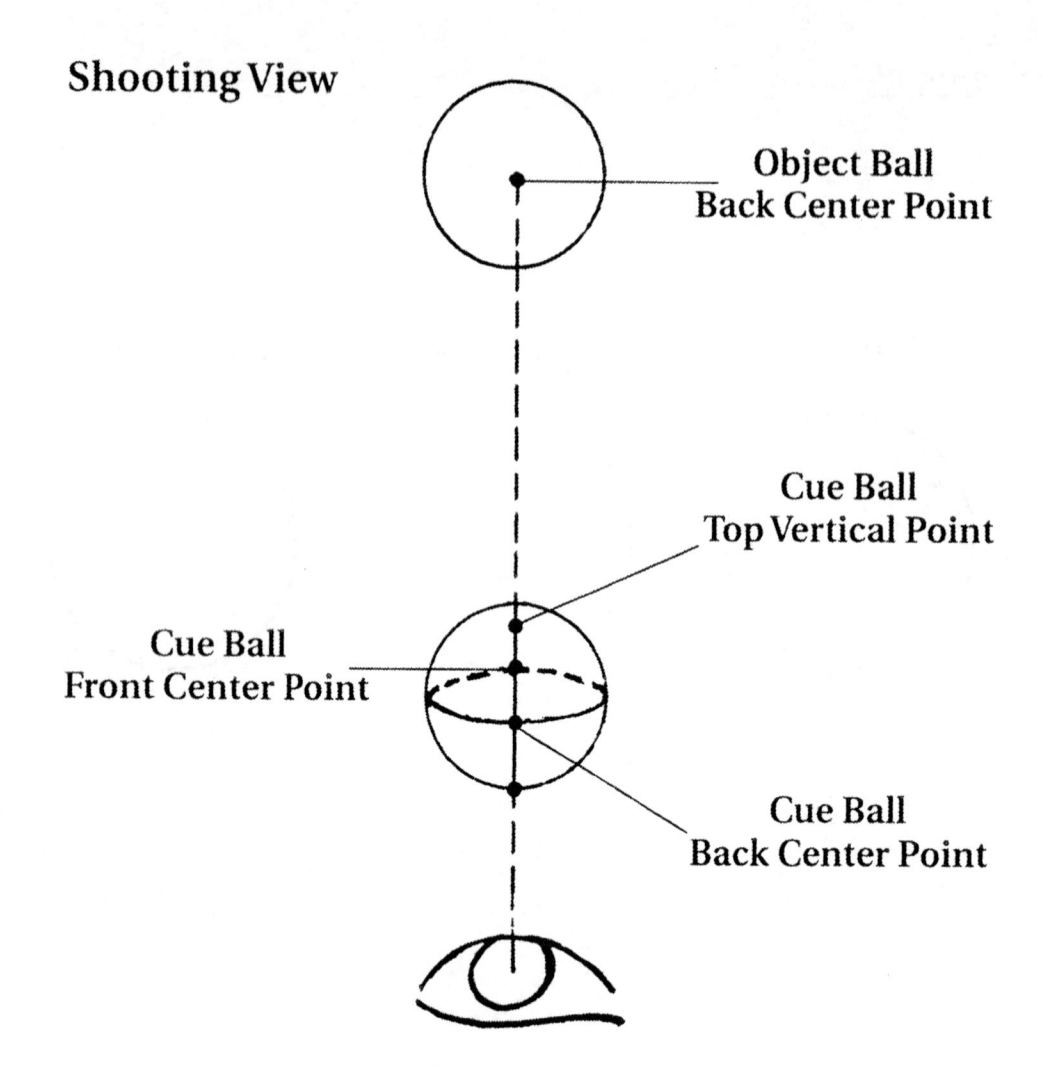

Whole Cue Ball Centerline

Note: As you can see, the reason there is no need for an aim compensation, **when you are directly over the aim line** with a Pure Eye in the Rifle Shooting Alignment, or when your Two Even Eyes are aiming from the Nose Center Alignment). This is simply because **the Back Cue Ball Center Point will be aimed on the same straight Cue Ball Centerline as the Front, and Middle Cue Ball Center Point**.

*The Front, Middle and Back Center Points form the whole Cue Ball Centerline!

For the longest time, I tried to equate what I had learned in grade school with aiming the **Cue Ball**. I was taught that a round object and a spherical object have only one center point. (That is still true till this day, as far as I know). So, when it came to aiming a **Cue Ball**, I naturally transferred this spherical fact of having only one **Cue Ball Center Point** at which to aim.

So, I thought that the **Back Cue ball Center Point** was that "only" **Aim Center Point**. Eventually, I learned that there is a difference in aiming the **Front** or **Back Cue Ball Center Point** with a **Pure Eye, Two Even Eyes** and a **Dominant Eye from an off-center position.** But in my early pioneer days, it just never entered my wildest imagination to check to see if there may be a difference in aiming each one of them. I assumed a center point meant a center point!

After realizing that the difference in the distances between the Back Center Point and the Front Center Point would yield a different sight angle to each one from the off-centered eye(s), I then deduced that the cue ball would travel to two different targets on the pool table. Even if the two center points were slightly apart, it would make a big difference when shooting the longer shots. I couldn't wait to compare the two slightly different **Cue Ball** traveling results on the pool table.

The following illustration will prove the importance of aligning the Front, Middle and Back Center Points together, rather than just selecting one of them by themselves.

Illustration 51

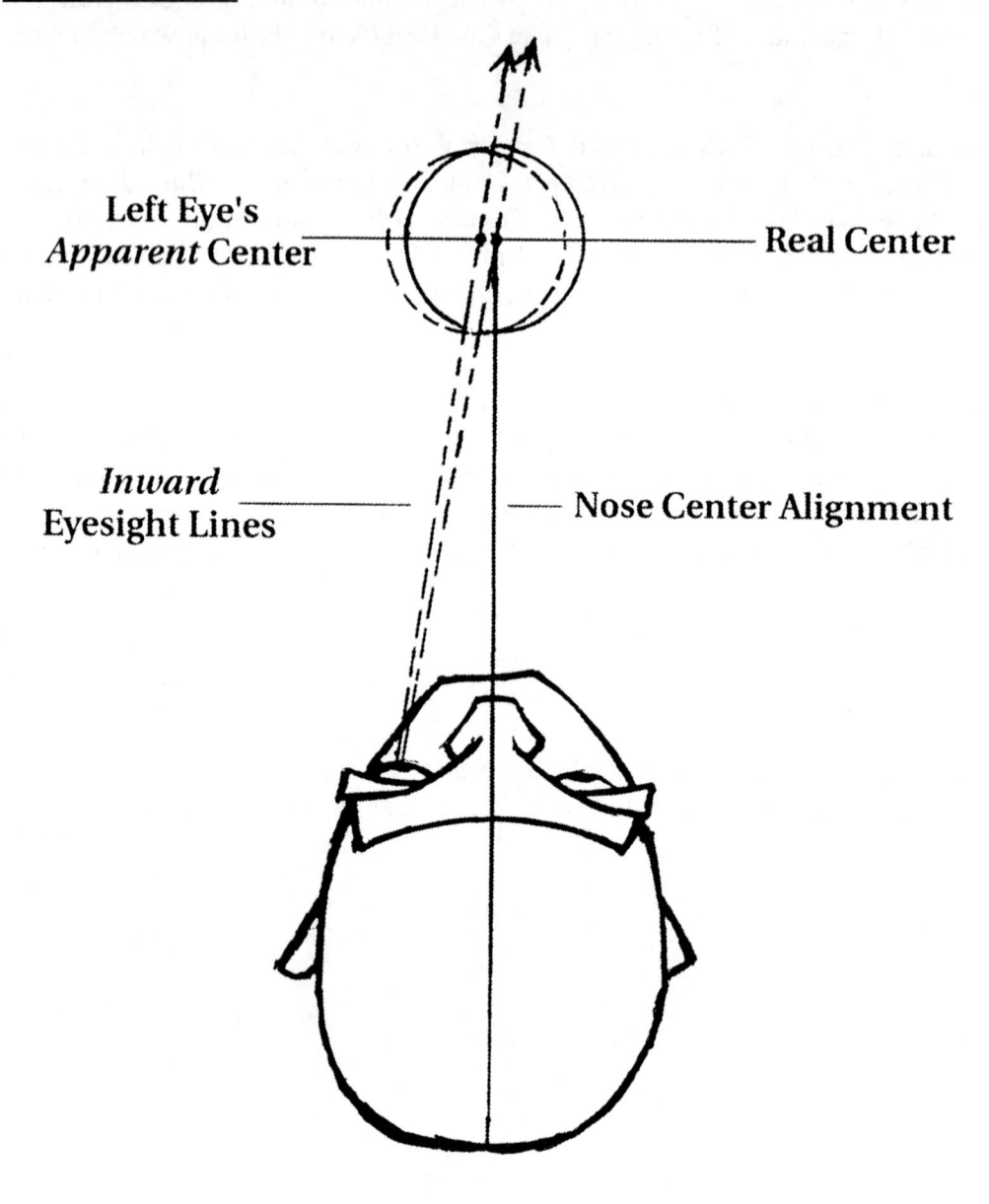

Note: Because of the out-to-inward line of sight, (the Left Pure Eye's aim from the Nose Center Alignment), the aiming of the **Real Front Center Point** resulted in a different rail contact point than the **Real Back Center Point**'s aim. (F is the **Front Center Contact Point** and B is **Back's Center Point**).

Also be advised that aiming the Top Vertical Point from an off-centered position will yield a direction between the Front and Back Center Point. Try it for yourself and see.

So, when using the Two Evenly Focused Eyes, draw the imaginary line from the **Front Cue Ball Center Point** through the Middle and Back of the **Cue Ball** with two evenly balanced eyes. **Be Careful!** Because, yes, it will be the **Nose Centerline** when you are in the **Nose Center Alignment**, but it might be located slightly different according to your turning and tilting of your head.

After you have calculated for the compensation, be sure to remain in the same alignment and use the same aiming eye(s) that you used to calculate for the aim compensation.

You can not move around in your alignment! You can not switch your *Aiming Eyes* around. Because, once you switch eyes or move your alignment, you will change your perception of the aim. **Once you move, you will need to calculate again!** Do you remember the switching of the eyes seemed to change the cue stick's alignment with different facial points?

Synchronized Peripheral Aim

Remember: Using the Two Even Eyes' Intersecting Aim with the Nose Center Alignment, or the Pure Eye's Straight Line of Sighting, or the Dominant Eye's *synchronized Peripheral Aim* requires you to aim the **whole** Cue Ball's Centerline (Front, Middle and Back Center Points) to the target!

Cue Tip Aim Compensation

Now that I have alerted those who didn't know that there is a difference between the **Real Center** and the **Apparent Center** for the cue ball and object ball, and, also that there is a need for aim compensation when using an off-centered aim/alignment, I will tell you that only half the battle is won. The other half is learning how to find and use the proper aim compensation to suit your personal needs.

Don't worry...Be happy! The other half of the aim battle strategy will be revealed in this and the following chapter!

Now, I would like to share with you a way *that will enable the shooter to shoot straight from an off-centered position.* It is for those shooters who choose to shoot from an off-centered position (for whatever reasons). And as you will see, it won't matter if you use A Pure Eye, A Dominant Eye, or The Two Evenly Eyes from an off-centered alignment. This method begins with the explanation of **The Real Front Cue Ball Center Point**.

In this chapter, I will show you the first "easy to use" method that I used when I aimed with a **Dominant Eye**, or any eye(s)' *off-centered aim/alignment.* It is based on stroking the center of your cue tip to the Real Cue Ball Center, while at the same time, aiming a specific cue-tip point (aim compensation) to your target. A little bit of trial and error is initially required. (Some learned pool players use this effective method).

When using the **Cue-tip Aim Compensation Points**, absolute consistency with your facial guide points (aligned with the cue stick) is a requisite. This is because your same **Aim Starting Point** must be a habit for **your** particular **Cue-tip Aim Compensation Point** to work!

So, by beginning the aiming of each shot by aligning your face to the cue stick before or at the same time, you actually begin to focus on the cue ball, aim line and object ball, you will be setting your face and eyes in a consistent angle for the start of your aiming process.

The secret: **once you start to focus on the cue ball, or the aim line, you can move your head vertically, but you can not move your head sideways!** *If you move sideways, even slightly, while you have your eyes fixated on an object, you will be changing your **Aiming Eye's Angle of Sight** with your face and the object.* And as a result, you will end up with a different alignment and a different line of sight from your face than what you started with.

Illustration 52

Real Cue Ball Center Point

Cue Tip Compensation Point

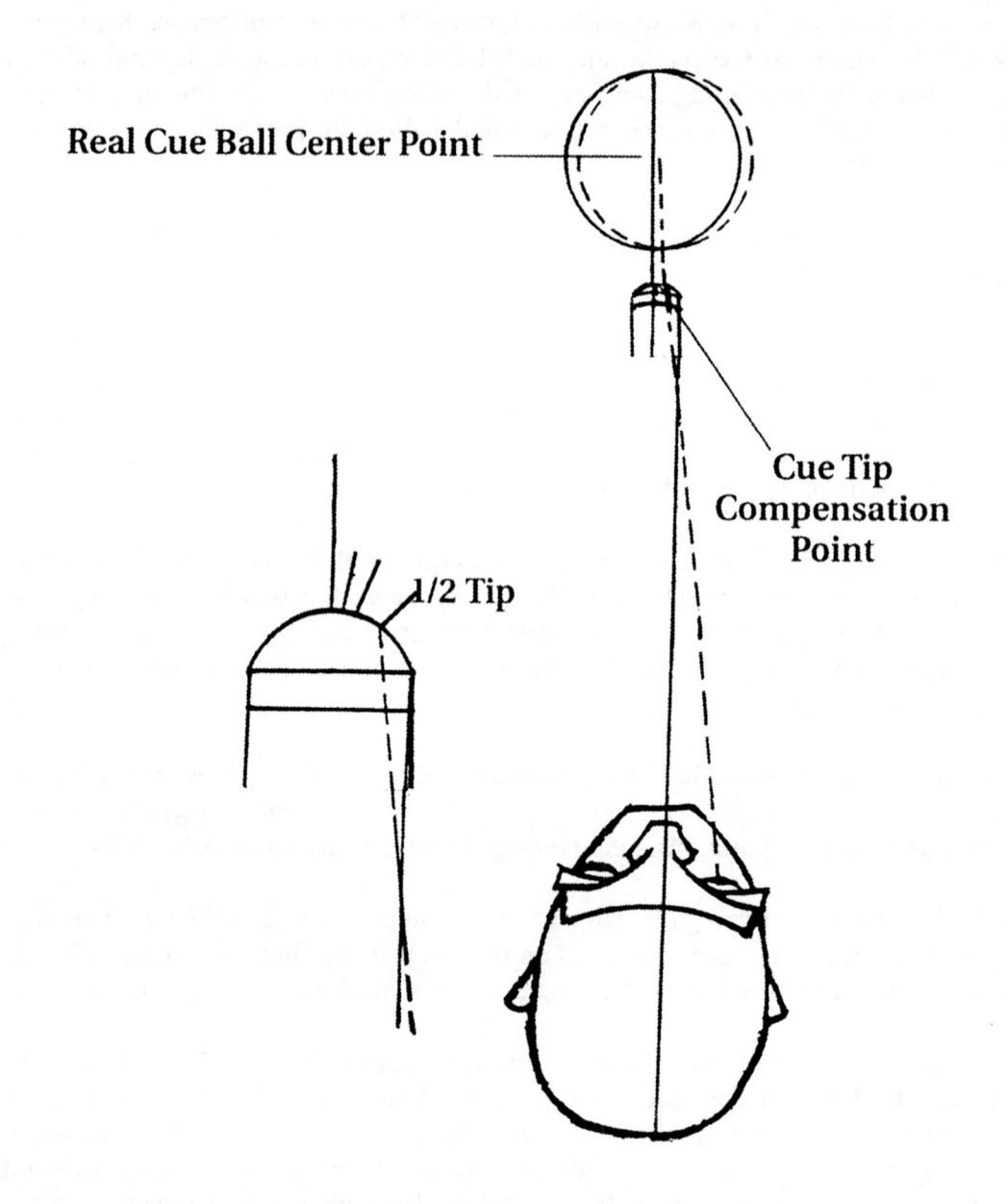

1/2 Tip

½ Cue Tip Point

Note: To start your trial and error process, **be careful to actually align the Real Centers of the cue and cue ball for all shots**, *but remember you will be aiming the cue tip aim compensation point to the object ball point or target*!

In this attempt, I started with the cue-tips "Right ½ Point" for the **Right Pure Eye** with the Chin Center to the right cue tip edge. **If that does not work for you**, then try the ¼ point, and then the 1/8 point, etc. (After aligning my Left Chin Edge to the Right Cue Edge, **I use my Left Pure Eye to aim through the Cue Tip and Cue Ball Centers!**)

Starting the aim process with the **Right Pure Eye,** but with a different **Aiming Starting Point** (the Chin's Left Edge to the cue stick's edge), results in a <u>different</u> **Cue Tip Aim Compensation Point!** (See below).

Illustration 53

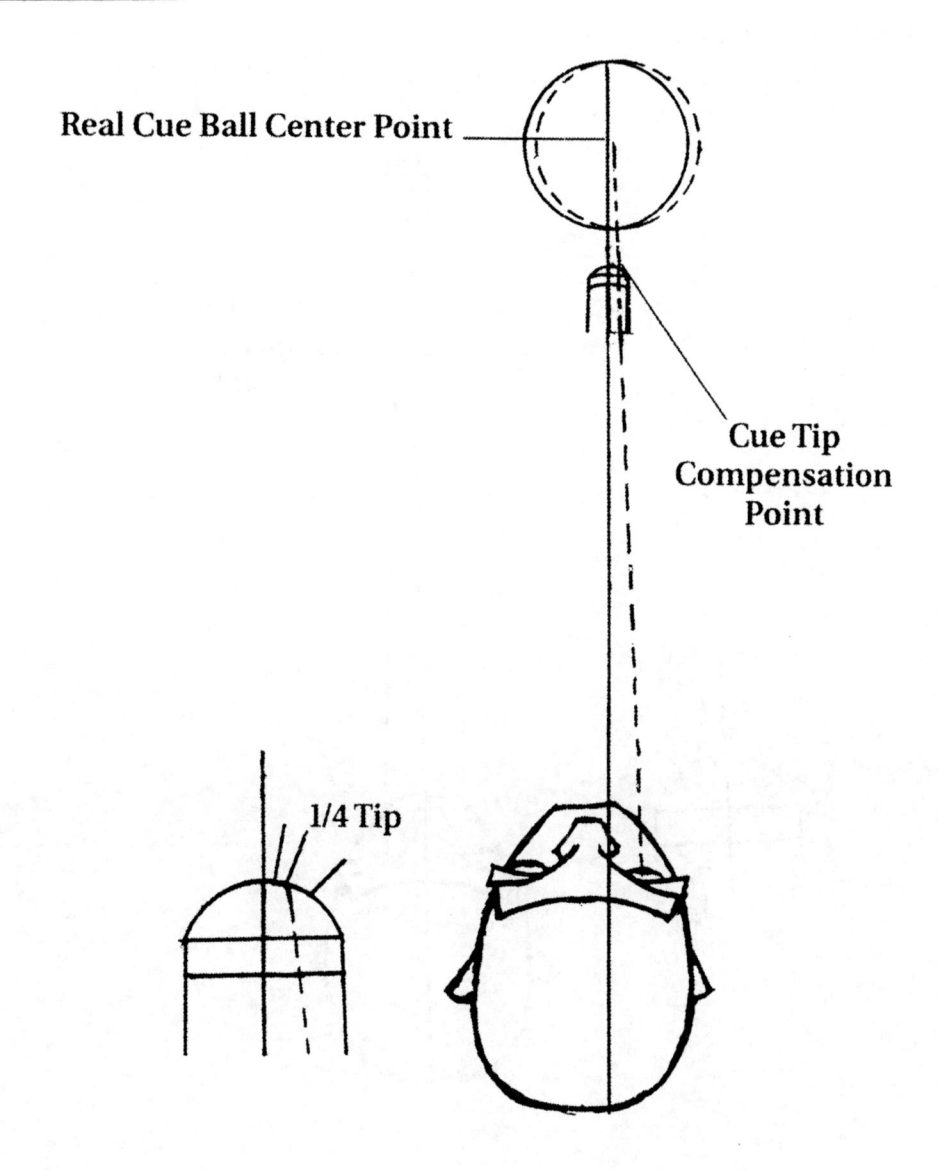

Real Cue Ball Center Point

Cue Tip Compensation Point

1/4 Tip

¼ Cue Tip Point

Note: In this example, the shooter has started focusing on the cue ball when he aligned the cue stick's "**Left Edge**" with his Chin's "Left ½ Point". He is using the **Right ¼ Cue Tip Point** for aim compensation. Some of you may find that for this particular alignment another cue-tip's point will work for your **Right Pure Eye!**

Illustration 54

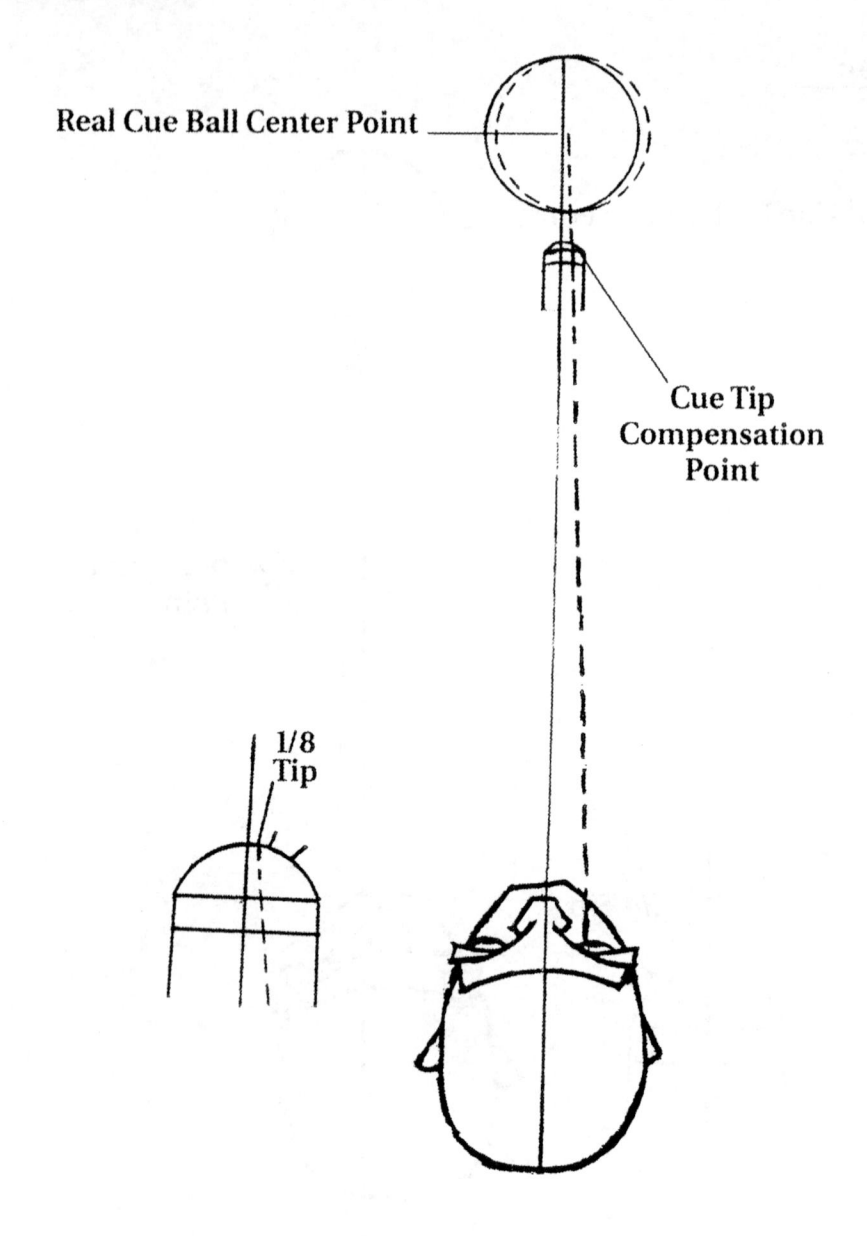

1/8 Cue Tip Point

Note: In this example, the shooter has started focusing on the cue ball when he aligned the ***cue stick's center with his Chin's Center***. He found that for this particular alignment, he sees that the cue-tip's **"Right 1/8 Point"** works for his **Right Pure Eye from the Nose Center Alignment!**

As you begin to focus on the cue-tip and cue ball, you will randomly select a cue-tip point to start with, then continue selecting until you find the correct cue-tip point that will work for <u>your</u> particular alignment over the shot.

As you might imagine from just these examples, depending on the various alignments, there are many different cue tip points that can be used for your **Cue Tip Aim Compensation Points**.

The different **Cue Tip Aim Compensation Points** depend on the person's physical make-up, their particular head angle (as a result of the amount of turn and/or tilting). This also applies to their **Aim Starting Points**, the various **Facial Points** over the various cue stick points, and the eye aiming preference (a **Dominant Eye, Two Even Eyes**, or a **Pure Eye**).

Applications

Now, let's learn how simple it is to apply the Cue Tip Aim Compensation to the **Double The Distance Aim Method**. However, the second one - **The Ghost Ball**, or **The Imaginary Cue Ball Center Method** - will need something different.

With the two aim methods that I will show, you will be basing your aim on the Cue Ball Center for all shots.

How many of you aspiring pool champions tried the Straight Shooting Test again, after learning about the Cue Tip Aim Compensation. If you didn't, why don't you try it now? Go ahead and see what a difference it makes.

Cue Tip Compensation/Double the Distance

All right, starting with the **Cue Tip Aim Compensating** when using the **Double the Distance Aim Method**:

The first observation you will make is that you will be starting your first aim to the object ball's desired contact point with the **Cue Tip Aim Compensation Point** instead of with the **Real** or **Apparent Cue Ball Center**.

The second observation you should make is that, after you calculate the distance to be added to the **Object Ball Contact Point**; you will be aiming with the **Cue Tip Aim Compensation Point** instead of with the **Real** or **Apparent Cue Ball Center**. (No illustration is needed here. Just remember to start and finish your aim with <u>**your appropriate Cue Tip Aim Compensation pointed to the target in each step**</u>).

Look at the following illustration.

Now, the **Imaginary Cue Ball Aim Method** needs something... a little different. (Gaze on the illustration below).

Illustration 55

Imaginary Cue Ball Center Point

Object Ball

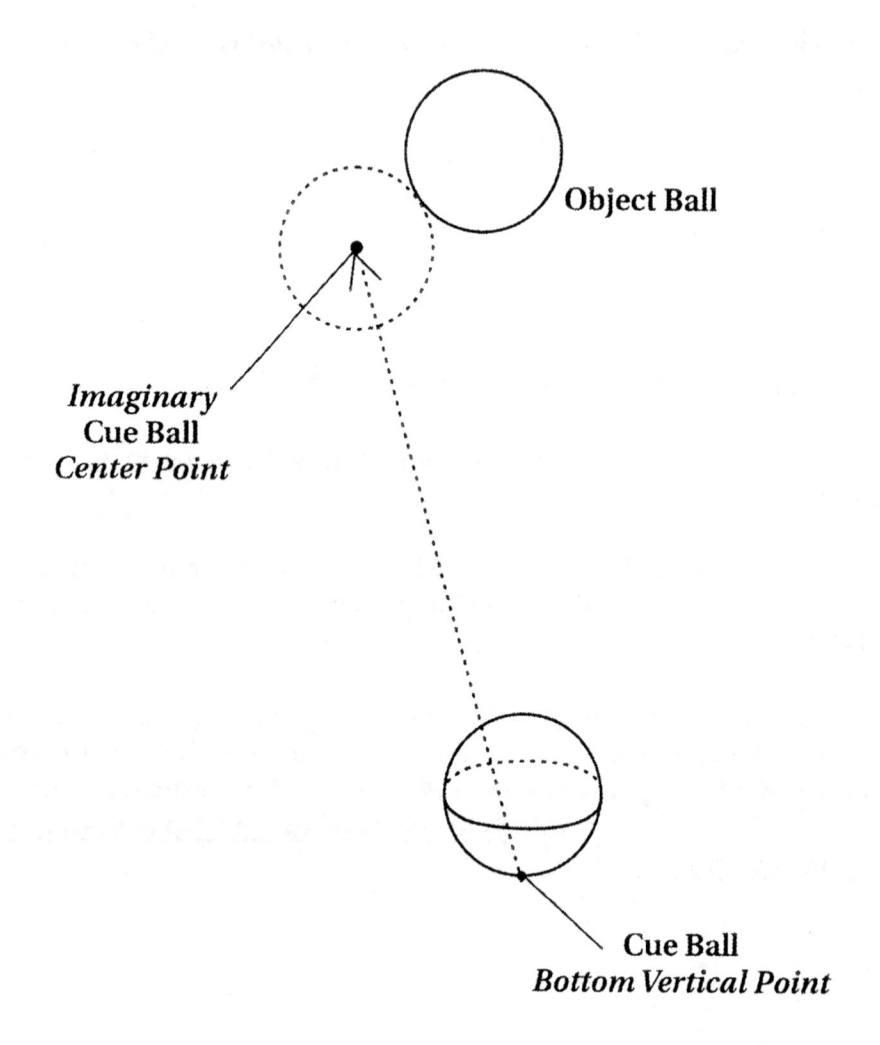

Cue Ball *Bottom Vertical Point*

Imaginary Cue Ball/ Vertical Bottom Center Point

Note Well: The *Cue Ball's Vertical Bottom Center Point is aimed at the Imaginary Cue Ball Center Point on the tablecloth*. (The **Vertical Bottom Center Point** is the *lowest point* on the cue ball as it lies on the table).

Why do you suppose that this is the point to start the aim compensating instead of from the **Front Cue Ball Center Point or Top Vertical Point**? It's because it is the same Cue Ball Point that will <u>contact</u> the **Imaginary Cue Ball Center Point** on the table!

Alignment

My following suggestion will help you to determine when your alignment with the shot is straight. Make a note (mentally and on paper) where your **Top, Middle** and **Bottom Facial Guide Points** align with each other when you are in a straight aim over your target. This way you will know how all three of your **Facial Points** should align with each other. So, then, if you see that your established **Top Guide Point** is not aligned with established **Middle** and **Bottom Guide Points**, you will recognize that your alignment is *off*.

If you see or feel that your alignment is *off*, check to see if your head and cue stick is supposed to be straight! I say this, because during your searching for your most comfortable alignment, you might have unknowingly aligned your head over the aim line with a "slightly turned or tilted head". In this case, you might have a "slightly to the right - **Top Point**" aligned to a "slightly to the left - **Bottom Point**". (Right and left points are based on having the nose as the **Center Point**).

STRIVE FOR ALIGNING WITH A STRAIGHT HEAD FOR ALL YOUR ALIGNMENTS! For one thing, it will help to keep your eyes on a "vertical track" when adjusting your aim between the cue ball and the target. Another thing is it will make the finding and using of your Facial Guide Points much easier to use as a peripheral aim aid.

There is nothing wrong with aligning with a head that is not precisely straight, as long as you can consistently aim and stroke straight! So, if you are not in comfortable alignment, get up and start over!

Aiming

Now, for aiming to a target, you start your alignment with your **Eyebrow or Nose Point (Top Guide Point)** in line with the imaginary aim line. Your **Top Point** should be "*peripherally*" above the cue ball, as you focus on the whole shot (cue tip, cue ball and the target point).

Try to angle your head comfortably, downward enough, so that the target and the **Eyebrow Point** are close enough to be peripherally seen together. (By angling your head downward you will be bringing the **Top Guide Area** closer to your target).

If your face is angled too high, it will be harder to *peripherally* compare the target with your **Top Guide Point**, because they will be farther away from each other. (Knowing this will aid in shooting the long shots).

Note: If you see that your **Top Guide Point** is not precisely aimed to your target and you know for sure that you have the cue stick aligned correctly with your face, then move your aim, until your **Top Guide Point** is aimed to the target, while you keep your face and cue stick in the same position with each other. The common mistake committed in this situation is to only move your cue stick or readjust the face/cue alignment while searching for the correct aim. Once you have the correct face/cue alignment, you should adjust your aim without disturbing it!

Use the **front Cue Ball Center Point** to start your aiming process. Simply move your face's position to the right or left (depending on your Right or Left Aim Eye) until you see that the **Front Cue Ball Center Point** is in line with the **Middle** and **Back Cue Ball Points**.

Aim Starting Tip: Begin your aim process by fixating your eye(s) on the Front Cue Ball Center Point. Then move your face's alignment until you see that the Middle and Back Points are directly in line, too. ***This simple adjustment* will prove to be an integral key to most Straight Shooting Deficiencies!**

Be careful with not confusing the **Apparent Centers** for the **Real Centers** on the Cue ball and Object Balls. Remember that being off-center is the root of the **Apparent Center!** The **Dominant Eye** is a **Two Eye Aim** that is off-centered! Thus, it is very easy to mistake the **Apparent Center** for the **Real Center** when using a **Dominant Eye Aim**!

Parallel Aiming

I would like to introduce one of my several Aim Methods. As you will learn, it can be used with the *off-centered Pure Eye*, the *off-centered Dominant Eye* and, even, the *off-centered Two Even Eyes*! I call it "***Parallel Aiming***".

As you will see, the eyesight aim lines are not out-to-in angled or in-to-out angled, or directly over the Cue Ball Center. The angle of the sight lines will *parallel* your Nose Centerline, and, if it's a straight shot you're shooting, the eyesight line will *parallel* the Cue Ball and Object Ball Centerline. (See below).

Illustration 56

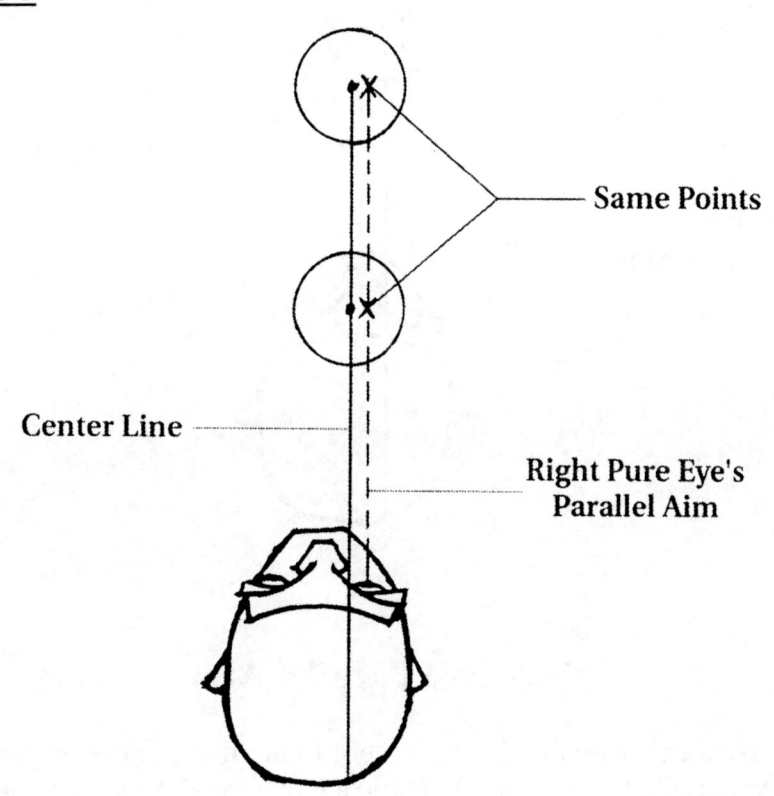

Note: This Straight Shot set-up shows the shooter's **Right Pure Eye** *paralleling* his Nose Centerline which is directly over the Cue Ball and Object ball Centerline. Thus, the shooter's eyesight line *parallels* the Centerline of the Cue Ball and Object Ball, as it passes through the same exact Cue Ball and Object Ball Contact Point!

99

Illustration 57

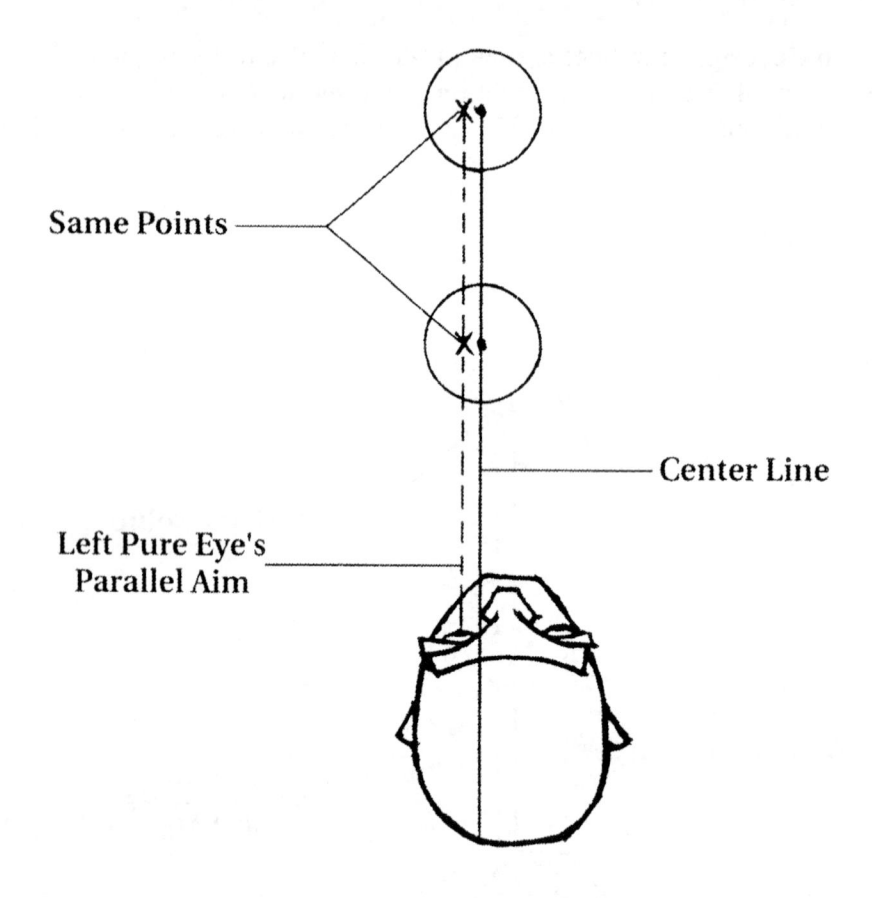

Same Points

Center Line

Left Pure Eye's Parallel Aim

Pure Eye Parallel Aim

Note: In the above example, the shooter's Nose Centerline is closer to the Cue Ball/Object Ball Centerline. As a result, the shooter's **Left Pure Eye's Straight Line of Sight** is also closer. The shooter's parallel line of aim passes through the same Cue Ball/Object Ball Contact Point!

As you can imagine, there are many off-centered alignment positions for a *Parallel Aiming Eye*.

Illustration 58

Side A   Side B

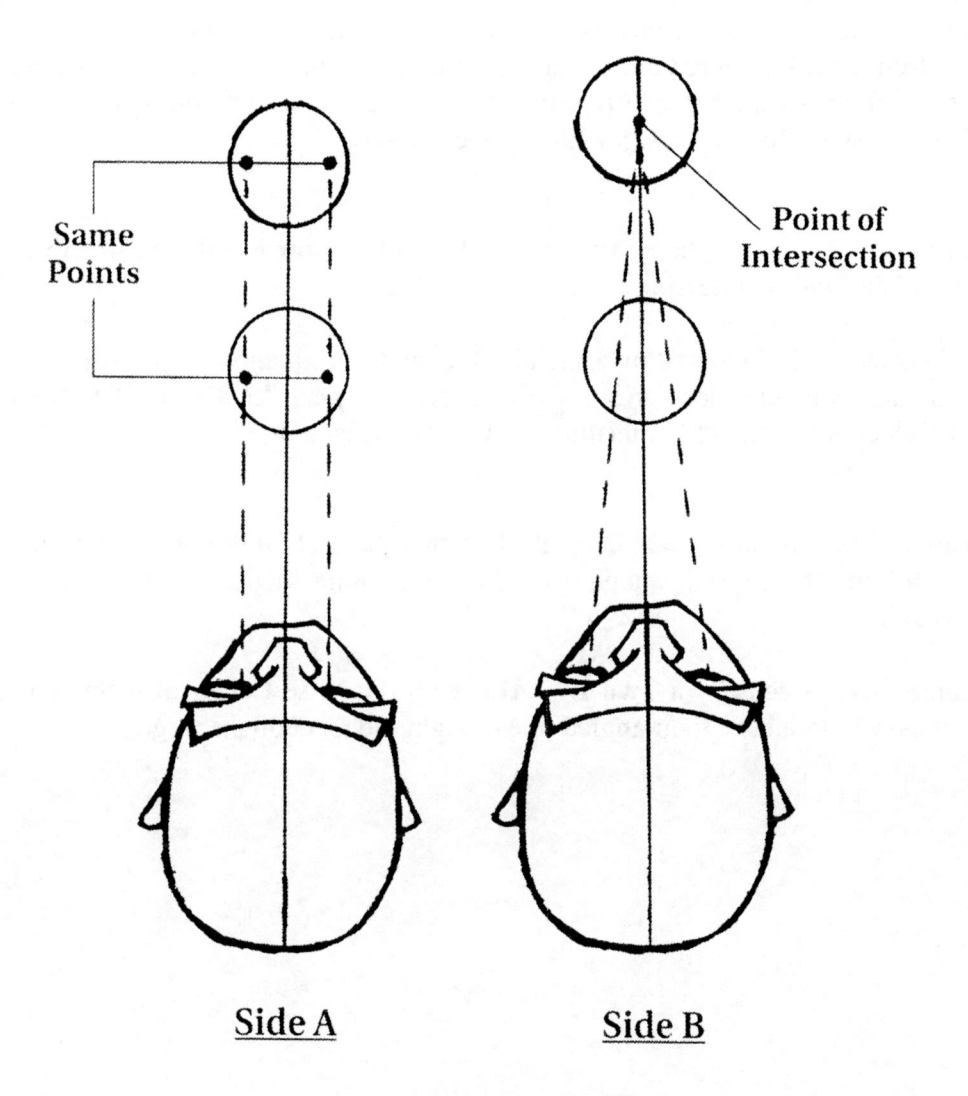

Two Eye parallel Aim

Note: The two illustrations above are showing the shooter in a Nose Center Alignment. Side A has his both eyes *parallel* his Nose Centerline and the Cue Ball/Object Ball Centerline. Side B has him *intersecting* his **Two Evenly Focused Eyes** on the ball center.

You can also apply the **Two Eye Parallel Aim** when your Nose Centerline is not centered over the Cue Ball Center, too! Remember that the key in *Parallel Aiming* is a **Straight Head** (Vertical with Aim line and Cue Ball Center).

So, here is a quick summary for the **Two Evenly Focused Eyes**, the **Pure Eye** and the **Dominant Eye Aim**. Even though, you will probably settle on using only one, I strongly recommend that you become familiar with all **Eye Aims**. You never know when you might want or need to change. (***Knowledge is power***).

The **Two Evenly Focused Eyes** can 1- *intersect* their balanced aim on the target from a **Nose Center Alignment** with the aim line and use no aim compensation. 2 – *Intersect* their balanced aim on a target from an off-centered alignment and use aim compensation, or 3 – *Parallel* their two lines of sight from a centered or off-centered alignment and aim through the same **Cue Ball/Object Ball Contact Points** (thus, no aim compensation).

The **Pure Eye** only has a straight eyesight line! With a **Straight Head** the **Pure Eye Line of Sight** will *parallel* the **Nose Centerline**.

The **Pure Eye** can be 1- Centered over the aim line and use no aim compensation. 2 – Off-centered and use aim compensation, or 3 – Off-centered and *parallel* it's aim line through the same Cue Ball/Object Ball Contact Point (thus, no aim compensation).

The **Dominant Eye** has no straight eyesight line that parallels the Nose Centerline or aim line. With the **Dominant Eye**, one angled eyesight line is more focused on the target than the **Inferior Eyesight line.**

The **Dominant Eye** is actually a **Two Eye Aim** with the Nose Center off-centered, but the shooter's two eyes will both have their angled line of sight intersect on the target.

WARNING !

DANGEROUS

CURVES

AHEAD !

LOOK OUT BELOW !

I have something to show you, which was an unnoticeable ingredient in my shooting inconsistencies for some time. I was unconsciously making a regular and costly mistake when I would try to locate the required object ball's contact point when shooting a 'cut shot'. The reason for this mistake was my eyes **Standing Angle**, as I looked down over the *spherical shaped* pool ball. It is because of my *looking down* on the object ball that my judgment in locating the actual object ball **Equator Line** deceived me. (Take a look at the illustration below).

Illustration 59

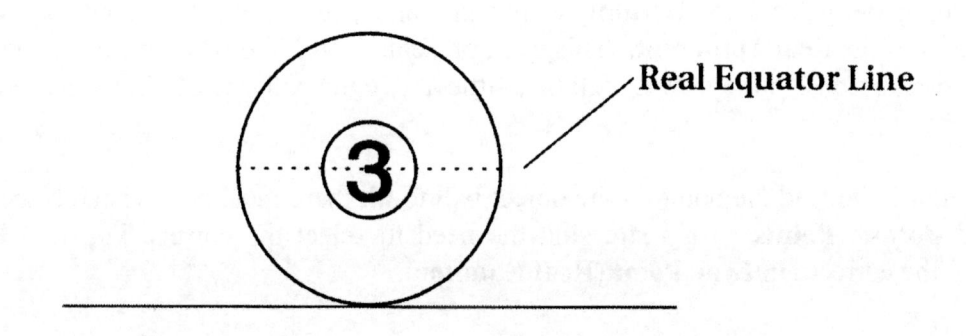

Real Equator Line

Illustration 59 is a table level view of an object ball with it's **Table Level Outline** and it's **Real Equator Line** represented by the dotted line.

As you can see from a table level view in Illustration 59, there is little trouble in correctly judging the **Table Level Equator Line** of the object ball's contact point. (The **Real Equator Line** is where the object ball and cue ball's contact point resides).

Apparent Top/Bottom Points

I am saying that the difficulty arises, in "visually bisecting" the correct **Bottom** and **Top Points** to get the **Equator**, when in a standing position. The flaw occurs when you use **Apparent Top Point** with the **Apparent Bottom Point** where the pool table cloth **seems** to touch the bottom of the spherical ball. <u>This is not the **Real Top** or the **Real Bottom Point** of the ball</u>. The *Real Top* is the *highest point* from the table's surface, and the *Real Bottom* is the *lowest point* touching the table.

Real Top/Bottom Points

Remember: The shape of the pool balls has a *'curving'* feature, so you won't be able to actually see where the bottom of the ball touches the table. Your **Standing Angle** prevents your eyes from seeing the ball's **Real Bottom**, while ignorance, or carelessness contributes in the wrong selection of the Real **Top Point**. This even presents a problem when we are down in our shooting position, because our eyes will still be a little above the ball's **Table Level Equator.**

NOTE: In order to find the point on the object ball to hit there must be a 'visual bisecting' of the **Top** and **Bottom Points**. I am stressing the need to select the correct **Top** and **Bottom Points** to find the correct **Halfway Point (Real Equator)**.

Take a good look at Illustration 60 on the following page.

Illustration 60

Table Level Top
Standing Top
Standing Bottom
Table Level Bottom

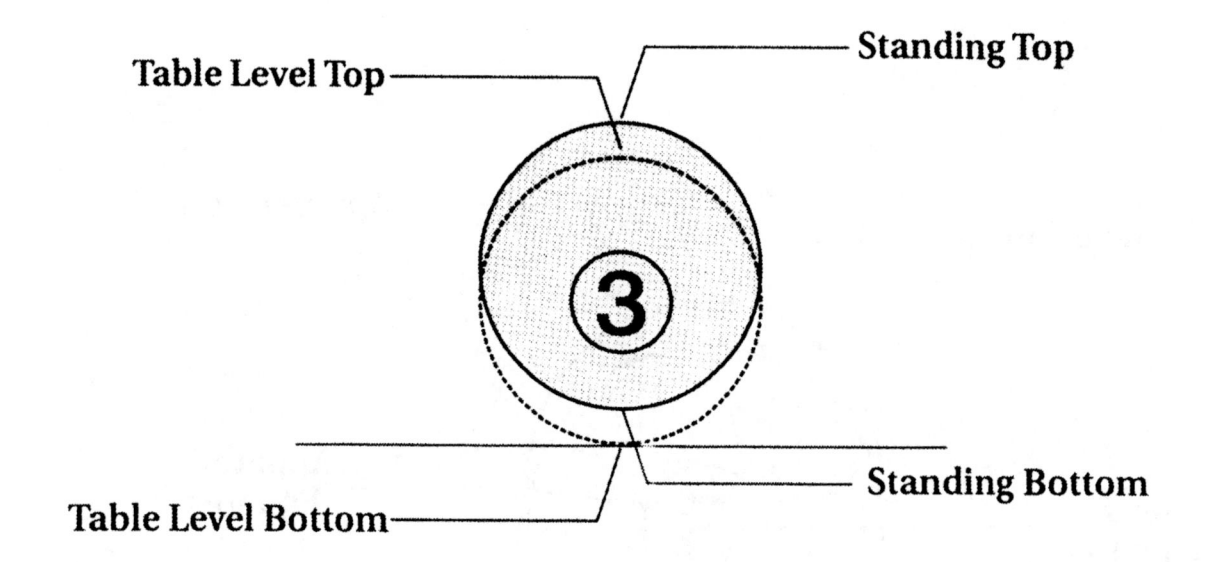

Standing View

The above example is a **Standing View**, as you look down on the same spherical shaped pool ball.

Notice the shaded and dotted areas drawn on the pool ball. The dotted lines and shaded area show a combined **Standing and Table Level View** of the same ball.

> The area between the *dotted* outlines represents the area on the pool ball, which you see from only a *Table Level View*.

> The area between the **Standing Top Point** and the **Table Level Top Point** represents the 'extra' amount of area that I will see because of my *Standing Angle*, as I look down on the spherical shaped pool ball.

Notice that from the **Standing Position** you can not see the **Real Bottom** of the object ball touching the cloth, but what you do see in the top view, which you don't see in the **Table Level View** in Illustration 60, is the shaded area which is showing more of the back area at the top of the ball.

Illustration 61

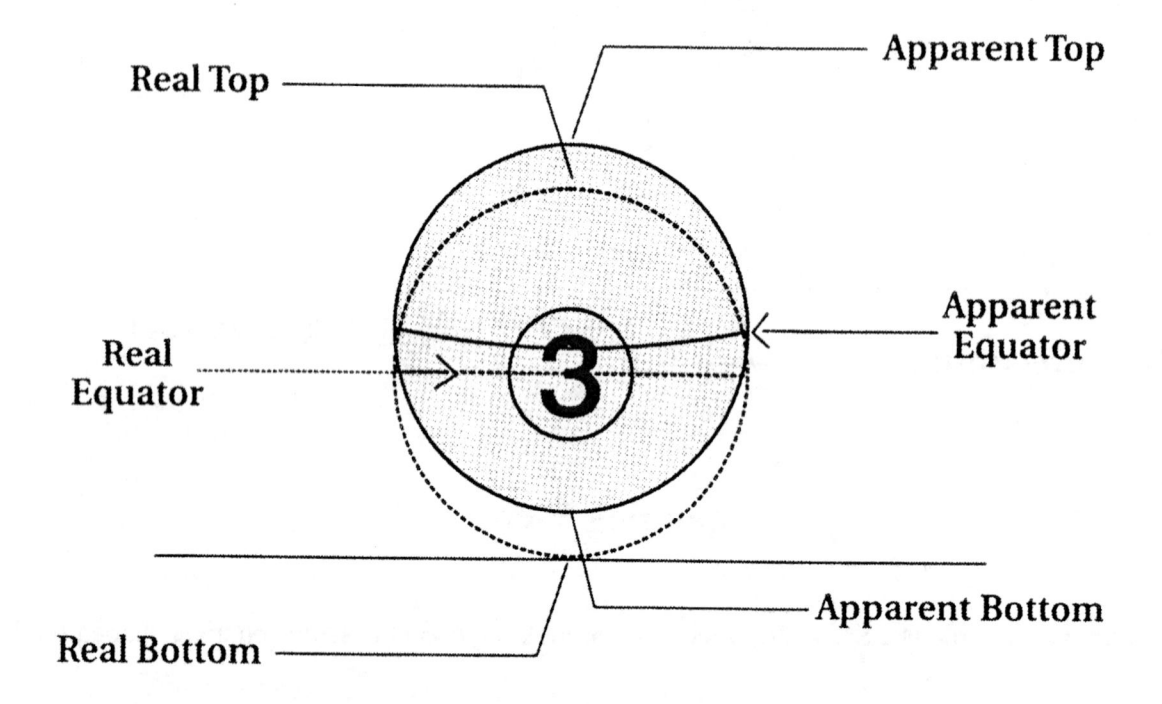

The example shows you what I call the **Apparent Top** and the **Apparent Bottom Points**, as seen from the **Standing View** while the *Real Points* are the **Table Level Points**.

Note: You can see a little arcing on the Apparent Equator from a looking position that is higher than a table level view.

In the previous illustrations, you will notice that as you look down from a **Standing View**;

The **Apparent Top Point** is higher than the **Table Level Real Top Point**.

And the **Apparent Bottom Point** is also higher than the **Table Level Real Bottom Point.**

Conclusion: **Apparent Points** are 'higher looking' when compared with the **Real Points** from the standing position's **Looking Down Angle**.

Apparent Equator Line

So! What is the significance in showing you the error in selecting the contact point from the object ball's **Apparent Equator Line**? **To alert you to this subtle aiming mistake!**

Apparent Object Ball Contact Point

Let me explain how I was unknowingly committing this error. In order to find the required contact point, I stood directly behind the object ball, and then sighted down the required aim line, from the object ball to the center of the pocket. Then, as I moved behind the cue ball without flinching my focus, I calculated my aiming adjustments based on that same exact **Apparent Object Ball Contact Point.**

Visual Bisecting

Do you understand? The mistake was that I started my aim with an **Apparent Object Ball Contact Point**, which is *located above the real contact point*. I was doomed, even before I began aiming the cue ball, because the "*Visual Bisecting*" must be between the **Real Top** and the **Real Bottom Points**, in order to get the **Real Contact Point**!

So, what about you? **Are you locating the Object Ball's Equator based on where you guess you are seeing the Bottom of the ball touch the table, as well as, where you think the Real Top Point is located?** It's the looking down view that will cloud your perception in locating the **Equator Line**.

Take a look at the following illustrations showing what happens to the object ball's travels when I pick the contact point from the **Apparent (wrong) Equator Line**.

Illustration 62

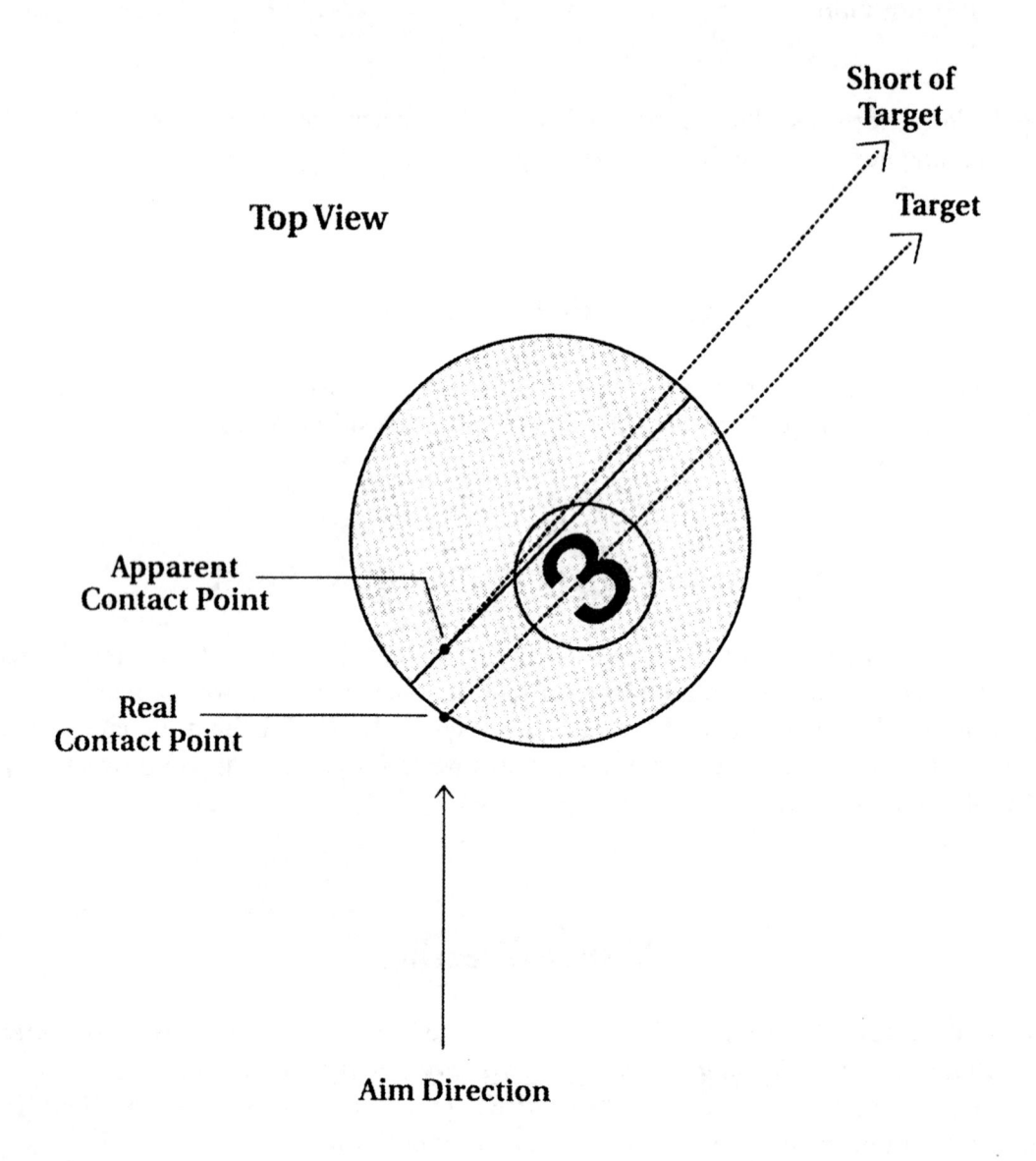

Top View

Short of Target

Target

Apparent Contact Point

Real Contact Point

Aim Direction

Note: As a result of picking the "higher" ***Apparent Object Ball Contact Point*** (Contact point on the **Apparent Equator Line**), I am hitting the object ball *fuller* than I want. Thus, the object ball will travel **'short'** to the target.

*The same "short of target", also results in selecting the contact point *below* the Real Equator Line!

So, as a result of my visually bisecting; the **Apparent Top and the Apparent Bottom**, or the **Apparent Top and the Real Bottom**, or the **Real Top and the Apparent Bottom**, I will err in my calculations for the *Real Contact Point.*

*The simple fact is that the **Real Equator Contact Point** extends *wider* than any other higher or lower point on the spherical balls! (The table level side view in Illustration 59 shows the **Real Equator's** protrusion the best). *I was missing shots because I was not cutting the object ball wide enough*!

As you have seen, this subtle error in judgment will definitely result in the cue ball and the object ball contacting at a different contact point than planned.

I know that all the players do not judge the **Object Ball's Contact Point**, as high as I am showing in the last illustrations, because **players of different heights will see the *precise location of the Real Equator Line* differently**. This is due to the origin of their eyes in their different **Standing Angle**s over the spherical balls. The higher your eyes are above the ball's equator, the sharper their descending angle is to the ball's contact point below. I am exaggerating this calculation to make it easier to show you what happens when the wrong **Equator Line** is selected in place of the required contact point.

Remember that selecting the wrong equator point also applies to the bottom half of the **Real Equator Line**!

Illustration 63

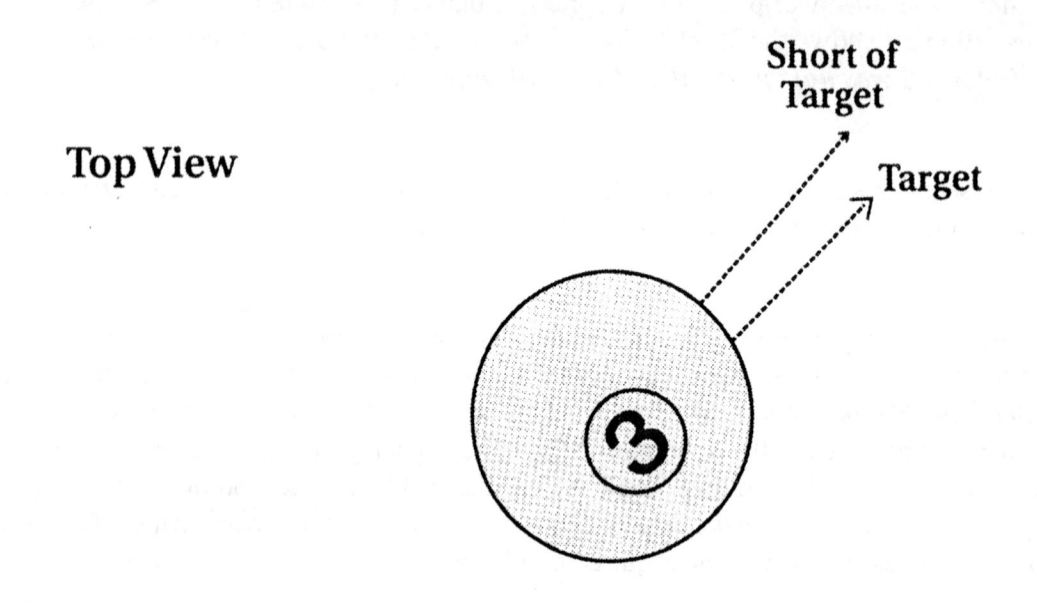

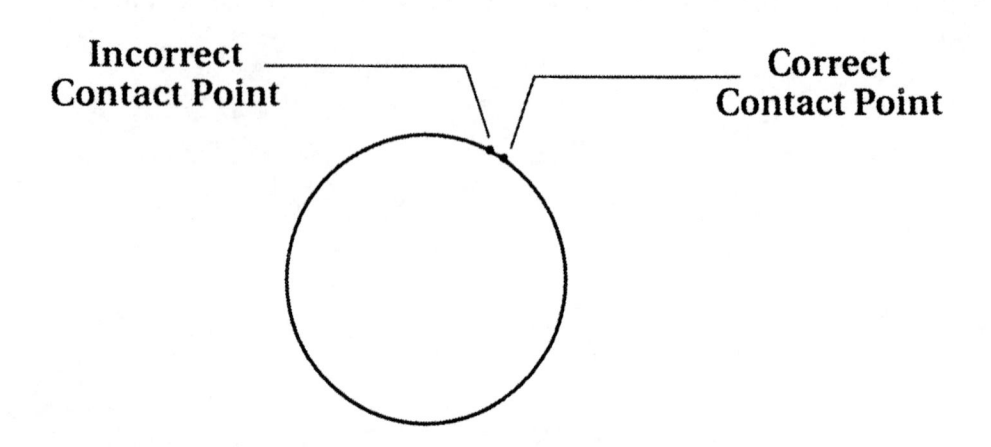

Top View

Short of Target

Target

Incorrect Contact Point

Correct Contact Point

Note: In the above illustration, I am using the **Contact-to-Contact Method** to cut the object ball into the pocket. The **Object Ball Contact Point** location on the **Real Equator** is correct, misjudged the *curvature* of the cue ball's top outline area. I did not align my eyes directly over the cue ball contact ball and, as a result, I incorrectly judged the cue ball contact point from an off-angle!

Here is another fine flaw during the process of aiming, which is related to the pool balls being spherical. Look at the illustration below.

Illustration 64

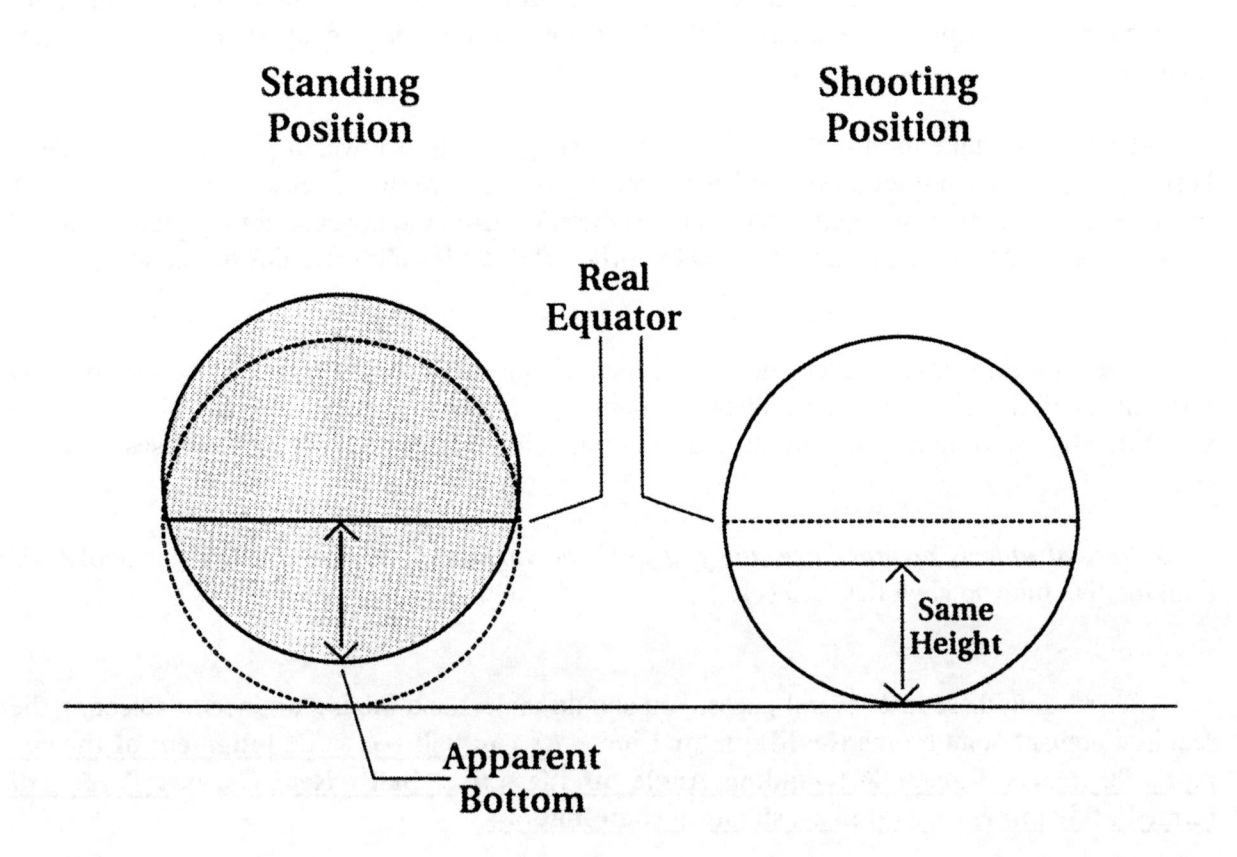

Standing Position   **Shooting Position**

Real Equator

Same Height

Apparent Bottom

Below the Real Equator Line

Note: After I estimated the distance between the **Real Equator Line** and the table cloth from my Standing Position, I **incorrectly** established this distance (height between the cue ball's **Apparent Bottom** and **Real Equator Contact Point**), as being **unchanging** for all the *varying heights* from which my eyes will look during my aim process. As a result, I am aiming *below the Real Equator Line* and will come "short" of my intended target.

The proper selecting of the **Real Equator Line also applies to the Cue Ball.** You will be wrong with your hit, if the object ball's contact point is correct, but the cue ball's is wrong.

The mistake occurs when you are in the process of comparing the object ball and cue ball. As you switch your focus from ball to ball, you lower your head and eyes to your normal shooting height, and only look for the **Object Ball Contact Point** based on memory (locating the same height above the tablecloth), as you remember it from the initial higher angle. But in reality, as you lower your head, the **Real Object Ball Contact Point** will slightly increase its distance away from the tablecloth. (*This slight difference will make a big difference in pocketing balls*).

Let's say, in the previous example that from your **Standing Angle** the initial distance between the Real Contact Point and the **Apparent Bottom Point** looked to be about ¾-inch. If you commit the error in selecting the **Object Ball Contact Point**, you'll be looking for the same 3/4-inch distance from the bottom of the tablecloth while you are at your lower shooting position.

Whereas, you take the time to look again, when you're in a lowered position, the distance between the **Real Contact Point** and the table cloth will look to increase from 3/4 to 1 inch distance from the lower shooting angle. This is, because from the lower shooting angle, you will see more of the bottom area, while the **Real Contact Point's** location remains the same.

These subtle mistakes which did not happen all the time, or all at once, were extremely difficult to find. As a result of them happening sporadically, these hidden mistakes were intermittently 'shorting-out' my aiming process -- and blowing many of my mental fuses, as well.

Spherical objects do not have any flat exterior surfaces. So, do not aim the pool balls thinking that they do have flat surfaces.

After reading these last several pages, you should understand the importance of selecting the required contact point on the **Real Equator Line**. <u>**As you will see, your judgment of the cue ball's 90 degree Carom Rebounding Angle off the object ball's Real Contact Point will immediately improve, as well as, shooting combinations**</u>.

Make it a habit of always selecting the **Object Ball Contact Point** from the **Real Equator Line**, even when you find it necessary to aim the object ball to a specific side of the pocket for cue ball position purposes. (This is referred to as "Cheating the Pocket").

Sometimes, to insure that you are selecting the correct contact point from the **Real Equator Line**, before a game, stoop down and take a look at the object ball from a table level view and pick out the **Real Equator Line**. And as you stand up, continue to focus on the **Equator Line**. Once in the regular standing position, take a mental photograph of the distance that you are from the ball and where the **Real Equator** looks to be from your particular **Standing Angle**.

    This is important because the appearance of the **Real Equator Line** will change, as you move closer or further away, or if you stoop lower than normal. And that is why a taller or shorter player cannot see the **Real Equator Line** appearing on the same spot, because of their difference in their locations to the ball. So, be aware of the distance you are from the balls when you are judging the location of the **Equator Line**.

    And remember to Look Out BELOW the Apparent Points!

"My husband was so impressed with Richard's abilities and potential that he set aside time to spend with Richard. I know Willie would have been proud and glad to see the results of this informative work."

Mrs. Flora Mosconi
Wife of the legendary Willie Mosconi

"It's commendable to see someone take this aspect of the game and break it down to such a level."

Jerry Briesath
Dean of the Billiard Congress of America's
Master Instructors.
Best pool teaching reputation in the world.

"Answers To A Pool Player's Prayers contains unique and practical information to help you improve your personal game. I highly recommend it to players of all levels who are looking for new challenges."

Buddy Hall
Hall of Fame Player

"I have read and seen the videos, dozens of aiming systems and 'How To' books for club players like me. Kranicki's system is the easiest to follow and the most effective system for the Beginning and Intermediate Players that I have ever seen."

Elmer Smith
Award Winning Writer
The Philadelphia Daily News

About the Author

Richard Kranicki is an author/actor/pool teacher who was born, grew up and still lives in South Philadelphia. At fourteen, he played semi-pro basketball. At sixteen, he played his first game of Pool. His pool tutors include Jerry Briesath and Don Feeney.

Two of his proudest pool achievements were to have the greatest pool player of all time – the late Willie Mosconi – consent to work with him on an instructional book and being the only author ever to receive the Mosconi endorsement. Another memorable moment was playing Willie in a Charity Event.

Richard is the author of a pool screenplay now being considered for a major movie film. And to add to his credits, he is currently researching more innovative ideas to teach "Cue Ball Speed Control" and "Cue Ball English Applications" for his upcoming books!